A TREATISE

ON

LIGHTNING CONDUCTORS;

COMPILED FROM

A WORK ON THUNDERSTORMS, BY
S. W. HARRIS, F.R.S.,

AND OTHER

STANDARD AUTHORS.

BY

LUCIUS LYON, A.M.

NEW-YORK:
GEORGE P. PUTNAM, 10 PARK PLACE.
M.DCCC.LIII.

PREFACE.

It is not a little remarkable, when we consider the prevailing disposition of the times to apply the discoveries of natural science to useful purposes, and to embody them in those material forms which make them subservient to the wants of man, that, among the books which are incessantly issuing from the press, none has yet appeared, in this country, exclusively devoted to the subject of practical electricity. Theoretically, indeed, the study of the phenomena of electricity awakens a lively interest in every mind, both on account of the wonderful developments which are constantly made, and the subtle and mysterious nature of its essence; seeming, as it does, to occupy the interval between mind and matter; but, since the brilliant experiment of Dr.

Franklin, identifying lightning with electricity, although much information has been acquired, both in this country and abroad, no treatise has been published, exhibiting to the American reader those facts which are necessary for his guidance, in applying the discovery of Franklin successfully to the protection of life and property.

The only explanation of this circumstance which can be given is, that the construction and application of lightning conductors, has appeared to most persons a matter too simple to need any aid from books, while not a few have looked upon the whole theory as absurd, and as a source of danger rather than of safety. There has been, consequently, but little encouragement for the compiling of a work calculated to bring before the community all that has been learned on this subject.

The various systems of rodding, however, which have sprung up of late, and the different modifications of the conductor, which have been patented and presented to the public, each claiming some peculiar advantage over all its competitors, have created a curiosity, if not a necessity, which seems to justify the publication of the present volume.

The valuable treatise recently published in London, from the pen of S. W. Harris, F. R. S., is quite too expensive to admit of general circulation; and it is thought, too, that one less extended will be better adapted to the wants of the American public. The compiler of the following work has, therefore, aimed to comprehend within reasonable limits all the facts that are essential, omitting such details as are merely curious, or such as suggest no new and valuable application of science. He has made a free use of all the materials within his reach, referring, for the satisfaction of the reader, as well as in justice to his authorities, to the book and page from which they have been derived.

There can be no doubt of the utility of such a book as is here presented. After expending large sums of money for the most approved apparatus of rods, many persons have been bitterly disappointed in their expectations, and have received no adequate return for their outlays. The truth is, that our countrymen have not acted on this subject with that shrewdness for which, in other things, they are proverbial. They have taken too much upon trust, and neglected the investigation of the facts. The iron conductors, put up at no inconsiderable cost, and supposed to secure perfect safety to the structures which they surmount, instead of proving themselves faithful sentinels and guardians in the hour of peril, have too often turned traitors, and invited the destruction which they promised to avert. The "swift fire of Jove, hurled by his red right arm," has not unfrequently bolted from the iron track, prepared for its harmless descent, and, indignant at some defective joint, or sudden break, or the want of sufficient metal for its free discharge, has made a forcible passage for itself, often leaving shattered walls, and chimneys, and blazing roofs, to attest its terrific power. Happy for the sufferers if the blasted corpse of some loved one has not added unutterable woe to the desolation of the scene!

Such disastrous consequences are due, in part, to imposture, but far more frequently to the ignorance and carelessness of workmen, and to the blind credulity of those who have employed them. In many instances, too, the owners of property have suffered an apparatus, originally well adjusted, to get out of repair. The distrust which might have arisen from these accidents, has no doubt been mitigated or prevented, in a great degree, by the difficulty of detecting any defect in a system of conductors—a philosophical knowledge of the science of electricity often being requisite for doing so.

Partly from the imperfections alluded to above, but much more from the unaccountable apathy which exists on the whole subject, a very large proportion of the owners of buildings in this country, and probably a still greater proportion in other countries, have neglected to avail themselves of the lightning conductor in any form. An incalculable amount of property, and many lives, which might be made at least relatively secure, are thus constantly and needlessly jeopardized. How great a risk is incurred, and how nearly absolute safety is attainable by conductors, the author hopes to demonstrate in the following pages.

Mr. Harris, in his unrivalled work on Thunderstorms, has the following appropriate Introduction:

"The fact of electrical conduction by metallic substances having been so long and so well established, any further discussion of the application of this principle to the purpose of protection against lightning may possibly appear to persons, conversant with such subjects, as in some degree superfluous. The damage, however, which so frequently occurs in thunderstorms, attended as it is with loss of life, and with serious inconvenience to the best interests of the country, may be fairly adduced as a sufficient reply to such an opinion.

"The beautiful spire of St. Martin's church, in London, has been recently rebuilt, at a cost of full one thousand pounds sterling, in consequence of an explosion of lightning, which fell on it in July last. Brixton church, near London, had also to undergo extensive repairs, rendered necessary from the same cause. In January, 1841, the spires of Spitalfields and Streatham churches, were struck by lightning, and the latter nearly destroyed; and in August of the same year an electrical discharge shook the spires of St. Martin's and St. Michael's churches, at Liverpool, both modern edifices of a costly and elaborate construction. In January, 1836, the spire of St. Michael's church, near Cork, was rent by lightning down to its very base; and in the following October the magnificent spire of Christ church, Doncaster, was almost totally destroyed by a similar discharge.

"Thus, in the United Kingdom alone, and within the short space of five years, we find at least eight churches to have been either severely damaged or partially demolished by lightning; to this list of casualties may be added the fine old church of Exton, in Rutland, which, according to the public journals, was in great measure destroyed in a thunderstorm, so lately as the 25th of last April. A writer in NICHOLSON'S *Journal of Science*, states that he has made a calculation of the average annual amount of damage done by lightning in England alone, and that it cannot be far short of fifty thousand pounds.

"In the British Navy the effects of lightning have been most disastrous. Since the commencement of the war in 1793, more than two hundred and fifty ships are known to have suffered in thunderstorms. It is not possible to state with any degree of precision the total amount of damage done, as all the instances in which ships have suffered cannot be well ascertained: some idea, however, may be formed of it from the following facts, derived from the official journals of Her Majesty's ships, deposited at the Admiralty. In one hundred and fifty cases, the majority of which occurred between the years 1799 and 1815, nearly one hundred lower masts of line-of-battle ships and frigates, with a corresponding number of topmasts and smaller spars, together with various stores, were wholly or partially destroyed. One ship in eight was set on fire in some part of the rigging or sails; upwards of seventy seamen were killed, and one hundred and thirty-three wounded, exclusive of nineteen cases in which the number of wounded is returned as 'many' or 'several.' In one-tenth of these cases the ships were completely disabled, and they were compelled in many instances to leave their stations, and that too at a critical period of our history. The expenditure in these few cases in the mere material, could not have been far short of one hundred thousand pounds sterling. So that if the whole amount of the loss to the public, in men, in money, and in services of ships, could be ascertained, it would necessarily prove to be enormous; more especially when we take into account the expense of the detention and refit of the damaged vessels, the average cost of a single line-of-battle ship to the country being one hundred pounds per diem and upwards. Now between the years 1809 and 1815, that is to say, within the short period of six years, full thirty sail of the line, and fifteen frigates, were more or less disabled.

"A very considerable portion of this mass of destruction occurred, it is true, at a time when a great number of ships were required; but at a more recent period, in time of peace, when the Navy has been greatly reduced, we find a large amount of these casualties to be constantly occurring. On the Mediterranean station alone, between the years 1838 and 1840, the *Rodney*, *Powerful*, *Ceylon*, *Tribune*, *Scorpion*, *Wasp*, *Tyne*, and *Blazer*, were struck by lightning, and many of them severely damaged: the *Rodney*, in addition to the destruction of her mainmast, was set on fire. In little more than twelve months, about the year 1830, three line-of-battle ships, a frigate, and a brig, were also more or less disabled. In other parts of the world we have lately had the *Rhadamanthus*, *Gorgon*, *Snake*, *Racehorse*, *Pique*, and many others, damaged by lightning; and in 1832, the *Southampton*, of fifty guns, narrowly escaped being blown up in the Downs.

"It has been suggested that many ships reported as 'missing,' have been destroyed in thunderstorms, a surmise almost converted into a reality, by the ravages which lightning is known to be capable of producing. From a reference to the official log of the *Lacedæmonian*, and to the evidence of Admiral Jackson, who then commanded her, it appears, that His Majesty's ship *Peacock* disappeared during a violent storm of lightning on the coast of Georgia, in the year 1814. The *Loup Cervier*, another of His Majesty's ships, was last seen off Charlestown, on the evening of a severe thunderstorm, and has not since been heard of. When

His Majesty's ship *Resistance*, of forty-four guns, was blown up by lightning in the Straits of Malacca, in the year 1798, two or three of the crew were picked up by a Malay proa, which happened to be in company; but for this circumstance, the fate of this ship would have remained in the same obscurity which now hangs over so many vessels reported as 'missing,' as all the rest of the crew perished.

"The journals of the ships of the Honorable East India Company furnish appalling statements of the damage and loss of life, caused by the electrical explosions which have fallen on them, while freighted with the rich products of the East: even so lately as 1842, the *Coote*, of twenty guns, one of the navy of this great mercantile power, had her masts shivered in pieces by lightning at Madras.

"Though we have not the same means of ascertaining the damage done to our mercantile marine, yet the loss to the shipping interest, in consequence of lightning, must be extremely great. Scarcely a year passes, without a calamitous account appearing in the public prints, of some fine merchant ship having been damaged or totally destroyed. In March last, the *Toronto*, one of the splendid packets which sail between London and New-York, was struck by lightning, which killed one of the crew, and damaged the vessel; and in August, 1842, the *Defiance*, a large transport laden with Government stores, including rockets and gunpowder, had her mainmast completely rent through to the keel by an electrical discharge off Nankin; the ship was filled with a sulphurous smoke, and the greatest consternation prevailed among the troops and seamen, from the dread of an immediate explosion. In May, 1840, the ship *Madras* was set on fire, and a portion of her side was driven out by an electrical explosion, and in 1839 a similar accident befel a large barque called the *John and James* off Algiers, so that she was with difficulty prevented from sinking. In 1838, the *Orwell*, a large trader laden with cotton, was set on fire, and narrowly escaped total destruction. Within a few years the merchant ships *Tanjore*, *Poland*, *Logan*, *Ruthelia*, *Bolivar*, *Boston*, and *Lydia*, are known to have been entirely consumed.

"However well, therefore, the fact of electrical conduction may be known,—however well scientific men may be agreed that, by the judicious employment of metallic bodies, we may ensure protection against lightning,—certain it is that the principle itself is far from being generally understood, or universally adopted. Indeed, to *existing* prejudices arising entirely out of a misapprehension of the laws of electrical discharge, may be traced the great destruction of life and property so frequently occurring from the effects of lightning.

"It is not easy to explain how, in the present advanced state of natural knowledge, so many anomalous views and opinions on this interesting subject should pervade the public mind, since in no department of physical science is the field of observation more fertile, or the path of experience more direct and certain. We have at our command the results of observation for nearly a century, during which time lightning rods have been employed; a great many instances are to be found, in which lightning has fallen on buildings under a variety of peculiar circumstances. In some cases lightning rods have been present, in others not: moreover, we can successfully imitate by artificial means the great operations of nature, and examine experimentally every probable result of a shock of lightning, and every possible contingency attendant on it. We ought, therefore, to find no difficulty in arriving at a practical solution of such questions as these:—Is the application of a lightning conductor desirable in any particular case? May it, by a species of attractive force inherent in it, cause a discharge of lightning, which, otherwise, would not have occurred in this particular direction? If so, may it occasion the damage it was set up to avert, through its inability to meet the explosion that may fall on it? Is it liable to produce destructive effects, by any species of lateral discharge of the electricity in passing along it? What are the best dimensions and form of a lightning conductor? and such like. If such questions as these cannot now be determined, they in all probability never will be."

Now if this unpretending volume, by attracting a more careful attention to practical electricity, and by diffusing in this community all the important information that has yet been elicited on this subject, shall be the means, under God, of preserving the property of any individual, or of preventing the loss of a single life, the author will feel that the time and labor devoted to its preparation will be amply compensated by the amount, however small, thus contributed to the sum of human happiness.

LUCIUS LYON.

CONTENTS.

SECTION I.

GENERAL VIEW OF NATURAL AND ARTIFICIAL ELECTRICITY.

SECTION II.

APPLICATION OF METALLIC CONDUCTORS TO THE DEFENCE OF BUILDINGS AND SHIPPING FROM LIGHTNING.

SECTION III.

RESULTS OF THE APPLICATION OF LIGHTNING RODS TO BUILDINGS AND SHIPS.

FROM THE PERIOD OF THEIR FIRST BEING EMPLOYED IN THE YEAR 1760.

SECTION I.

GENERAL VIEW OF NATURAL AND ARTIFICIAL ELECTRICITY.

Electricity considered in relation to common matter—Conditions of a Thunderstorm—Insulation—Charge—Conduction—Discharge, &c.—Identity of Natural and Artificial Electricity—Nature of ordinary Electrical arrangements producing Disruptive Discharge—Various Phenomena of Thunder and Lightning—Appearances termed Fire Balls—Sulphurous odor of the Electrical Discharge—Artificial discharges of various kinds—Luminous appearances similar to those in Nature—Further observations on Thunder Clouds—Electrical Discharges—Possible Causes of Discharge—Upward Discharge.

NATURAL

AND

ARTIFICIAL ELECTRICITY.

Electricity considered in relation to Common Matter.

BEFORE entering upon the subject of the application of metallic substances to buildings and ships, with a view to their protection from lightning, it may not be unimportant to review the amount of information we are in possession of, relative to the nature and operation of thunderstorms.

A large induction of facts, leaves little doubt of the existence of some elementary or primordial principle in nature, every where present, and intimately associated with the particles of common matter, according to some general law. In what this element consists, we are quite ignorant; we know, however, that there is such a constituent principle, and that it is capable of exerting, under given circumstances, an all-powerful action; hence it may be considered as a species of unknown physical force or agency, the laws of which it is our business to investigate.

Now it is no objection to the practical results of such an inquiry, to say that we are ignorant of the nature of the agency with which we are dealing—it being the great end of modern philosophy rather to trace, and apply the uniform relations of certain facts, than to speculate upon the nature of the mysterious causation, upon which the connection depends. Thus Newton was content to examine the laws of gravity, and the relations of this force to common matter, without in any way meddling with its nature as an occult cause; and from this method of inquiry the happiest consequences have resulted. The same method is equally applicable to the subtle principle active in a thunderstorm: we may arrive at all the practical information we require relative to this grand yet fearful display of its powers, even although we should never understand its nature as a primary source of causation.

This physical force or agency has been termed electricity,* and there is some strong evidence for supposing it to be an extremely attenuated and subtle kind of matter—differing, however, in its properties from any form of matter of which we have cognizance.

It is insensible to ordinary perception so long as it is distributed amongst the particles of bodies ac-

* The Greeks observed its effects in amber, ἤλεκτρον, hence the term.

cording to a given law. In this state it is said to be neutral, or inactive; when, however, the equilibrium of distribution is from any cause disturbed, then a variety of interesting phenomena begin to appear, and the electrical agency manifests a tendency to return to its previous state of quiescence.

A variety of natural and artificial operations affect the neutral electrical state of matter. Under natural operations, may be classed changes of temperature, changes in the form of bodies, chemical changes, &c.; thus brimstone, chocolate fresh from the mill, wax, resin, &c., when melted, become electrical in cooling; the tourmalin, also, and many other substances, evince electrical signs under a change of temperature. In the decomposition of water, by means of sulphuric acid and zinc, we find the bottle in which the chemical action is proceeding strongly electrical; and it is a remarkable fact, that during the progress of thunderstorms, the vapor of the atmosphere is condensed into rain, or frozen into hail, and the general temperature of the air altogether changed.

Hence, from the sum of our knowledge respecting meteorological phenomena, there appears great reason to conclude, that the causes which produce artificial electricity are all in full operation in the masses of vapor, among which natural electricity appears active.

This opinion is maintained by several eminent electricians of the present day. It was warmly espoused by the late Mr. Singer, who advanced in support of it the following positions: (1.) That the electrical phenomena of the atmosphere take place, in all climates, to the greatest extent, about the period of the greatest degree of heat, when the rays of the sun have caused a considerable accumulation of vapor. (2.) Where this cause operates to the greatest extent, as, for instance, within the tropics, natural electricity is produced on the largest scale. (3.) When the natural source of evaporation is assisted by collateral causes, electrical changes occur with astonishing activity, as in the eruption of a volcano, or the heat imparted to the air in its passage over large extents of hot sands, as those of Africa. (4.) By the action of winds, currents of air of different temperatures are often mixed, so that such as have been heated and charged with moisture, become suddenly cooled, thus occasioning a precipitation of water, and the occurrence of electrical changes. This is often witnessed on the coast of Guinea during the existence of the Harmattan. (5.) These electrical changes are every where most frequent when the causes of evaporation and condensation suddenly succeed each other.

After advancing several cogent arguments in favor of the above facts, and noticing, in a very candid manner, some objections urged against the theory they are intended to support, Mr. Singer concludes with the following truly appropriate and judicious observations:—" Although the immediate causes by which the various phenomena of the atmosphere are produced, be still far beyond our comprehension, yet the connection of their several effects is a sufficient demonstration that they are not purely mechanical, but subservient to the direction of supreme power and intelligence. By this means, the most simple arrangement becomes the source of sublime effects. The process of evaporation which modifies the action of the sun's rays, and conveys to every part of the earth's surface a source of fertility, does at the same time diversify the appearance of the atmosphere by an endless variety of imagery, enlivening the horizon with the most brilliant and glowing tints, and in all probability effecting those electrical changes which are the precursors of the most magnificent phenomena in nature."

Under artificial operations may be classed friction, pressure, and other mechanical actions:—the electrical machine, essentially a plate or cylinder of glass, made to revolve between or against fixed cushions, is sufficiently illustrative of this—we observe brilliantly luminous sparks fly round the glass, and dart off from a metallic substance opposed to it, in consequence of the disturbed state of the electrical distribution in these bodies.

Amongst the various relations of electricity to common matter, we find the following:—Some bodies facilitate the transmission of electrical action in so much greater degree than others, that they have been considered in the light of conductors of electricity; other bodies, on the contrary, admit of so little freedom in this respect that they have been denominated non-conductors, or insulators of electricity. The distinction, however, between conductors and non-conductors, although more or less arbitrary, may still be sufficiently defined for practical purposes:—thus all the metals more particularly may be taken as conducting bodies, whilst all vitreous and resinous substances may be considered as non-conducting bodies, or insulators. Hence it is, that we find the metallic conductors opposed to the cylinder of an electrical machine, supported on a glass pillar; by which the active electricity developed by the friction, becomes as it were imprisoned,—and accumulated on the metal.

It should, however, be clearly understood, that there are no substances which *perfectly* conduct or *perfectly* obstruct the transmission of electricity, their insulating or conducting power being only a difference in degree: still the differences are so great between various substances, that if classed in relation to such differences, those at the extremes of the series admit of being considered, the one as conductors, the other as insulators. Thus, while vitreous and resinous bodies admit of but extremely slow conduction, during which sensible and even considerable portions of time elapse, metallic bodies allow conduction to proceed with incredible rapidity. Professor Wheatstone, by a highly ingenious experimental process, has clearly shown, that the transmission of accumulated electricity through a copper wire, one-fifteenth of an inch in diameter, and about half a mile in length, proceeds at the rate of 576,000 miles in a second of time; supposing the electrical action to move from one extremity to the other; and that the light of the spark produced by it, has a less duration than the one-millionth part of a second.

The learned. Mr. Cavendish, in the course of some extensive inquiries into the electricity of the torpedo, found the difference between the conducting powers of iron and water, to be nearly in the ratio of four hundred millions to one; that is to say, electricity meets with no more resistance in passing through an iron rod four hundred millions of inches long, than it would meet with in passing through a column of water of the same diameter, only one inch long.*

TABLE *showing the order of the Conducting and Insulating Powers of various Substances.*

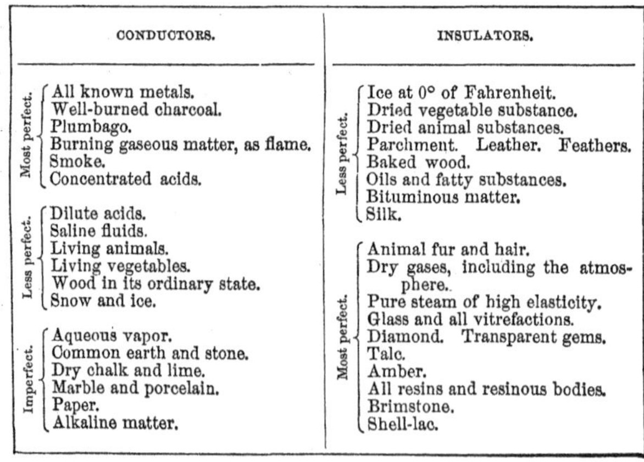

CONDUCTORS.		INSULATORS.	
Most perfect.	All known metals.	Less perfect.	Ice at 0° of Fahrenheit.
	Well-burned charcoal.		Dried vegetable substance.
	Plumbago.		Dried animal substances.
	Burning gaseous matter, as flame.		Parchment. Leather. Feathers.
	Smoke.		Baked wood.
	Concentrated acids.		Oils and fatty substances.
Less perfect.	Dilute acids.		Bituminous matter.
	Saline fluids.		Silk.
	Living animals.	Most perfect.	Animal fur and hair.
	Living vegetables.		Dry gases, including the atmosphere.
	Wood in its ordinary state.		Pure steam of high elasticity.
	Snow and ice.		Glass and all vitrefactions.
Imperfect.	Aqueous vapor.		Diamond. Transparent gems.
	Common earth and stone.		Talc.
	Dry chalk and lime.		Amber.
	Marble and porcelain.		All resins and resinous bodies.
	Paper.		Brimstone.
	Alkaline matter.		Shell-lac.

* *Phil. Trans.* for 1834, Part II.

If we arrange various kinds of substances in series, according to the comparative degree of resistance they offer to the transmission of electricity, we obtain the following order. The first column in the preceding Table contains the best conductors, and leads by degrees into the second column, in the order of their increasing resistance, until we arrive at the opposite extreme.

The order above given, is sufficiently near the truth: it is almost impracticable, however, to assign the exact place of some of the equivocal substances, more especially as their conducting power is liable to vary from many accidental causes. All charcoal will not conduct equally well, and some bodies which conduct badly as solids, will, by a change of temperature up to fluidity, become immediately conductors: thus ice at 0° of Fahrenheit is an insulator, but on approaching the melting point it becomes a conductor;—the conducting power of green vegetables, and raw meat, depends on the fluids they contain. The extremes of the series, however, are perfectly defined; if we commence with the metals we have the order of conducting power, and conversely, by commencing with shell-lac, we have the order of insulating power.

For the purpose of a greater degree of generalization, we may include, in the conducting class, all metals and metallic ores, acids, saline bodies, all fluids except oils, also stones and earthy matter, living animals and vegetables.

Under the insulating class, we may comprise all

resinous and bituminous matter, all vitreous matter, all gaseous matter, precious stones, dry animal and vegetable matter, silk and oils.

The following is an easy and simple experimental illustration of the conducting and insulating power of various bodies in respect of ordinary electricity.

Let a succession of sparks about two inches in length, continue to pass from the insulated conductor of an electrical machine to a metallic ball in connection with the ground. Apply now a stick of sealing-wax, or a dry rod of glass, to the conductor, no sensible effect will be produced on the current of sparks. But if the conductor be touched with a rod of wood, or put into communication with the walls of the building, the sparks will immediately cease, evidently showing that the accumulated electricity had been by these last substances carried off, whilst the wax and glass evinced no such power. In this way we may test the conducting power of the various substances above given, either directly, or by inclosing them in non-conducting tubes.

Although the distinction between conductors and non-conductors of electricity is to a great extent arbitrary, yet it is plain from the above facts, that such a distinction, in a positive sense, is quite admissible. Thus the substances commencing the first column of the preceding table, may be taken as being more especially conductors; those terminating the second, as obstructors or non-conductors of electricity: and the great practical fact which marks the distinction between them is this,—that the substances considered more especially as insulators, oppose such complete resistance to the transmission of electrical action, that an instantaneous return of the disturbance to a state of quiescence (p. 4), is *never* effected through them, without mechanical violence and displacement of their particles, without a vivid evolution of light and heat, and without producing at the same time, all the furious effects peculiar to an irresistible expansive force. The best conducting substances, on the contrary, yielding as they do almost immediately to the electrical transmission (p. 8), at once quiet the disturbance without any such disastrous consequences. The transmission through these is comparatively passive; and it is only in some few instances to be hereafter considered, that we find the small degree of resisting power they possess, productive of any ill consequence, and *then* only to the conducting substance itself, not to neighboring bodies.

Electrical conditions of a Thunderstorm.

We are indebted to Dr. Faraday's valuable and most interesting series of Inquiries in Electricity,* for very practical and sound views of the nature of electrical action. These we shall now proceed to apply to the conditions of a thunderstorm, which will serve at the same time to explain them.

A thunderstorm may be considered, as the result of a great electrical disturbance (pp. 4, 5), between

* *Phil. Trans.* 1831, to 1838.

masses of vapor condensed in the atmosphere under the form of clouds, a portion of the earth's surface directly opposed to these masses, and the intermediate air; the particles of which instead of allowing the disturbance to subside rapidly, virtually maintain it up to a point, at which its force is no longer to be resisted. For example; let the mass of vapor P P (fig. 1), under the form of a cloud, be

FIG. 1.

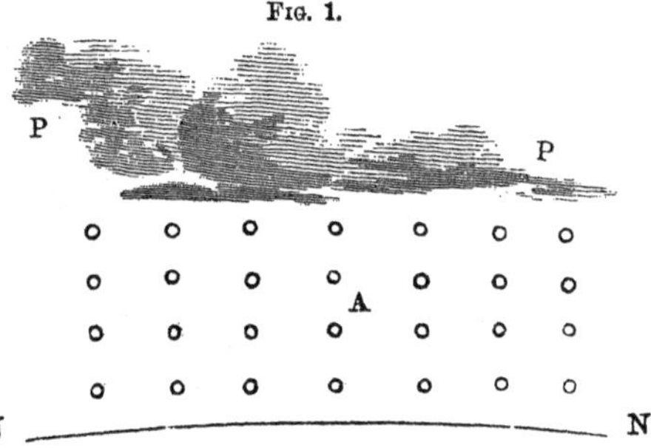

supposed to contain active electricity, in consequence of some of those changes in the condition of the atmosphere, to which we have already alluded (p. 5). Let N N be a portion of the earth's surface directly opposed to these masses; and A the intermediate atmospheric particles. Now, Faraday has shown, that in such a case as this, all these intermediate particles assume a peculiar forced electrical state, which he terms a polarized state. By way of typical illustration, let *a*, *b*, *c* (fig. 2), represent three of these consecutive particles, and suppose in their neutral condition the electrical distribution of each particle to be uniform and equal, as indicated by the equalization of the dark and light squares. Now, when these particles become placed under the influence of a thunderstorm, as represented in figs. 1 and 4, there would be no longer this uniform distribution. The electricity of the particles would be compelled to

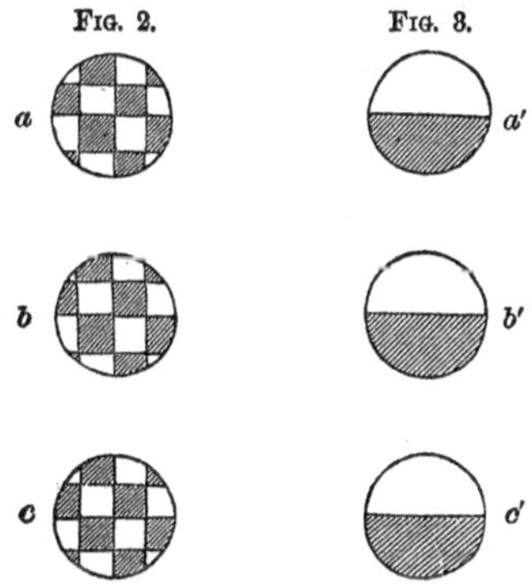

assume some new condition, such, for example, as that shown in fig. 3; that is, we may consider the electrical agency as being no longer distributed according to a law of quiescence, but to be, as it were, collected in the particle in some other way, according to a law of disturbance. Suppose this represented by the shadowed and light portions of the particles *a′ b′ c′* (fig. 3), the dense portions being constrained to appear in opposition to the light ones; and let us further imagine, that this state consists in a concentration of the electricity of each particle in one of its opposite faces: in this case the particles are said to be polarized.

The immediate consequence of such a forced state as this, is, that the electricity, rendered active by any of the causes above mentioned (p. 5), propagates through an insulating medium, such as the air, a species of disturbance from particle to particle, which at last arriving at distant conducting substances, elicits an active electrical condition of such substances, similar in effect to the primary disturbance, but opposite in kind. This Faraday shows to be the essence of that peculiar action of electrified on distant bodies, termed induction. Thus, assuming by way of illustration that P (fig. 4) were a cloud containing

FIG. 4.

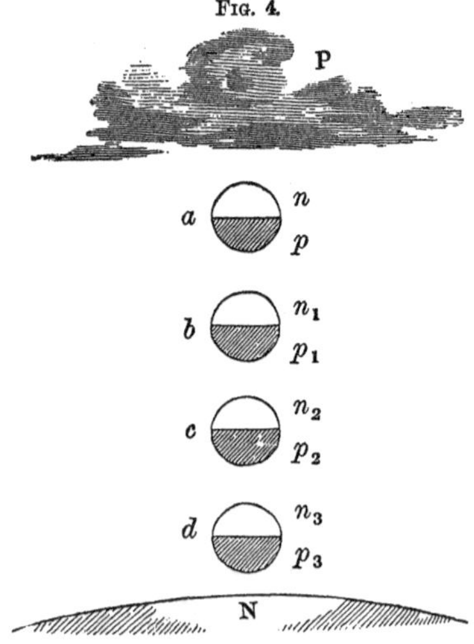

a greater quantity of electricity, than it could support in a state of quiescence, there would be immediately propagated through the intermediate particles of air *a*, *b*, *c*, *d*, &c., an induced action of this kind,—the intermediate particles *a*, *b*, *c*, *d*, would be constrained to assume the polarized state just mentioned. There would be, according to the principle we have just supposed, an alternate electrical condensation and exhaustion $\text{P}\,n$, $p\,n_1$, $p_1\,n_2$, &c., brought into play, which at last reaching the earth's surface, would there elicit an electrical force, N, exactly equal to the force at P, but of an opposite or neutralizing quality; so that there would arise at N, by this kind of action, an electrical exhaustion or displacement, just sufficient to tranquillize the active accumulation at P. Now it is of no consequence to the general result, which of these opposite states P, N be supposed to reside in the cloud P: we evidently may conceive the whole chain (fig. 4) to exist without any actual change in its condition, although the point N were imagined to be the state of the cloud, and P that of the earth: the intermediate particles *a*, *b*, *c*, *d*, would still become polarized in the same way, but in an opposite sense. We have only to conceive the figure reversed, and this will be immediately apparent, the conducting surfaces of the clouds and earth, being nothing more than the terminating planes of a great intermediate action, set up between them in a given direction.*

The induced disturbance at N, in the points im-

* Faraday has not unaptly termed insulating bodies dielectrics, and the media, through which induction is sustained, dielectric media, as expressive of substances through which electrical action is propagated from particle to particle.

mediately opposed to the electrical cloud P, may be considered as a species of reaction, and as giving origin to a new force. We have, therefore, in every disturbance of this kind, two forces present, exactly equal and opposite to each other. These opposite electrical states, have been imagined by some philosophers, to depend on the presence of two equally powerful, but dissimilar agents, termed the vitreous and resinous electricities, from the circumstance of one of them being very commonly produced by the excitation of vitreous, the other by the excitation of resinous substances. There is not, however, any essential difference between them, so far as relates to their action as physical forces; and although, for the sake of perspicuity, they may be considered as positive and negative powers, or as positive and negative electricities; yet it is still to be remembered, that one is as much a positive force as the other. It will be immediately perceived, that the two forces must necessarily exist both at the same time (p. 15) as at P, N (fig. 4): hence it is found impossible to charge common matter with one of them, without the other appearing somewhere, either in near or distant bodies,* just as it is impossible to pull against a fixed point, without eliciting in that point, an equal and opposite force.

Insulation—Conduction—Charge—Discharge, &c.

These points being apprehended, we are immediately prepared to receive the simple and lucid expla-

* FARADAY'S *Researches in Electricity*, p. 365.

nation, which this eminent philosopher has given us, of the terms, insulation, conduction, charge, discharge, &c.

We have already shown (p. 15) in what that peculiar and wonderful influence, termed electrical induction, may be said to consist, viz., a polarization, or forced state of material particles, by which an action is propagated, and made to appear in bodies however distant. This we have conventionally, or typically, represented in fig. 4, page 15; now supposing this state of the particles could be maintained under all circumstances, complete obstruction to the return of the opposite forces to a state of quiescence would be the result; and we should arrive at perfect insulation of these forces. This however is not the case, the constrained state of the particles *will not* remain, except for a limited portion of time. Thus in fig. 4, the positive force in P, will, if sufficient time be allowed, discharge into the negative force *n* of particle *a*, the positive force of this particle into the negative force n_1 of particle *b*, and so on to the negative force N, until the whole disturbance is quieted, and the polarization of the particles *a*, *b*, *c*, *d*, reduced. This process constitutes conduction, and it always proceeds more or less rapidly through every kind of substance; the more rapidly however it can proceed, the better the conducting power, and conversely, the less freely it can proceed, the more perfect the insulating power (p. 7).

Insulating bodies are, therefore, as already observed (p. 8), only conductors of a rigid and stubborn kind, the particles of which return to their normal state so slowly, that for a limited portion of time, they admit of being considered as exceptions to the general law of conduction; yet it is upon these bodies that the process of induction depends, and upon this process depends further, the state of things called electrical charge, typically illustrated in fig. 4. As long as the particles *a*, *b*, *c*, &c., can suffer the constrained state in which they are placed (p. 12), so long will the charge be maintained with but small loss; but when they can no longer resist the tendency of the opposite electrical forces P, N, to combine throughout the series, we have immediately what Faraday terms disruptive discharge—that is to say, the particles in fig. 1 (page 13), are displaced and broken through, with a greater or less degree of mechanical violence. In this case, the electrical disturbance in the particles having become as great as they can sustain, any tendency to further disturbance, instead of inducing further change, subverts the whole system, and a violent reunion of the opposite electrical forces instantly ensues.

Although such discharges are of a sudden and violent character, and productive of damage to bodies through which they pass, yet they occasionally become so modified by various circumstances, as to assume a more progressive and quiet form, often free from any attendant danger whatever.

If a pointed metallic rod, R (fig. 5), project freely into a charged system, P, R, N, from one of its terminating planes N, the polarized particles immediately at the extremity of the rod have the forced condition (p. 12) so highly exalted, that it terminates in discharge upon the next or more remote particles, the electrical condition of which is less intense. The consequence

Fig. 5.

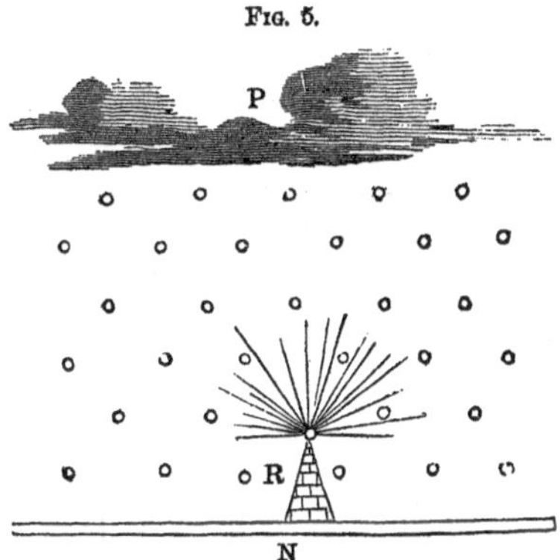

of this is, a luminous brush of beautifully colored light, attended by a sort of roaring noise. This brush discharge may be considered as taking place between a good and bad conductor: it is, in fact, an intermitting series of electrical sparks between metal and air; but in such rapid succession as to convey the idea of a continuous stream. The discharge in this case always commences at the root of the brush, and is complete at the point of the rod, before the more distant particles attain the same intensity: hence the discharge is progressive, and occupies a sensible time.

Brush discharge, by means of pointed or angular

bodies, will, under certain conditions of conduction, assume the appearance of a luminous star, especially when it is proceeding from a negative or resineus electricity (pp. 16, 17). Hence the observation, that electrical discharge *from* a pointed conductor, is attended by a luminous brush of rays, but *toward* a pointed conductor by a star of light.

When the air in contact with a metallic rod is becoming rapidly charged, we have another species of discharge, termed glow discharge; that is to say, the metal in contact with the electrified particles becomes covered with a glow of lambent light, producing a beautiful effect.

Dr. Watson, in the 48th volume of the *Phil. Trans.*, has collected out of ancient history several interesting notices of these electrical appearances. Thus Pliny, in his *Natural History*, tells us "stars settled on the sail-yards and masts of ships with an audible sound: also on the spears of soldiers." Seneca, again, in his *Natural Questions* says, that the "spears seemed to be on fire in the Roman camp."

Similar appearances are mentioned by Cæsar and Livy.

In more recent periods, we find repeated notices of similar natural phenomena. They are called by the French and Spaniards, St. Helmo's, or St. Elmo's fires; by the Italians, the fires of St. Peter and St. Nicholas. On ship-board in this country, sailors call them comazants. "In the night (says the Count de Forbin) we saw on different parts of the ship above thirty St. Helmo's fires; one of them was more than a foot and a half in height; its noise resembled that of fired gunpowder."*

Captain Waddel, of the merchant ship *Dover*, met with a heavy electrical storm in January, 1748: he says, "Sundry very large comazants (as we call them) settled on the spindles, and burnt like very large torches."† The ship was soon after struck by lightning. Captain Fanshawe, R. N., observed on board his Majesty's ship *Newcastle*, in May, 1821, luminous appearances "resembling the flame of a gas-light on the extremities of the masts; the lights were visible "sometimes on one mast, sometimes on another, and sometimes on all of them." The ship was sailing from Bermuda to Halifax, the weather unsettled and squally, with a "mass of black clouds close astern," vivid lightning and thunder occasionally.

At Plauzet, in France, the three-pointed extremities of the cross of the steeple, always appeared surrounded with a body of flame during great storms of lightning.‡

M. Toscan, the librarian of natural history in the Botanic Gardens in Paris, witnessed, in May, 1803, during the presence of heavy black clouds, a vivid glow of electrical light on a bent iron bar surrounding a wall in the gardens; it gave him the idea of a large ball of fire of a foot in diameter, and lasted eighteen seconds. This glow discharge pre-

* *Phil. Trans.*, vol. xlviii.

† *Phil. Trans.*, vol. xlvi. p. 3.

‡ PRIESTLEY'S *History of Electricity*, p. 273.

ceded a heavy stroke of lightning on the house about six feet distant.*

The fact of discharge occurring between bad and good conductors, in such way as to produce a spark, leads in some degree to an explanation of certain electrical explosions observed to occur, although rarely, in an apparently serene sky. Thus his Majesty's ship *Dictator* is said to have been struck and damaged by a fire-ball at Martinique, in the year 1794, during fine weather. In this case the surface of the sea may have discharged upon the nearest particles of air, which, by some of those changes so frequently taking place in the atmosphere had become polarized. It is not improbable, that on the same principle, luminous electrical discharges may occur between particles of polarized air in different states of intensity, producing those progressive appearances more especially called meteors. These have all the characters of a dense electrical discharge propagated, as it were, from particle to particle through a considerable space; and probably dragging into its path, light vapors and inflammable matter floating in the atmosphere, and increasing by their intense ignition the luminous and highly brilliant appearance which such meteors exhibit.

Identity of common Electricity with the agency of Lightning.

The years 1745 and 1746 mark an important

* Gilb. *Annal.*, xiii., p. 484.

era in the history of physical science. Von Kleist, dean of the Cathedral of Kamin, and some Dutch philosophers in the university of Leyden, in endeavoring to confine electricity within the limits of a small phial, discovered a method of accumulating it on glass to a most unprecedented degree, and of subsequently discharging it through bodies, in such a way as to produce the most powerful and astonishing effects. By these discharges a fearful sensation could be impressed on living animals—even life itself destroyed;—metallic substances could be violently heated, fused, and ignited;—inflammable bodies set on fire, and the most compact substances scattered in pieces, as if acted on by a violent expansive force. When, therefore, the cause of lightning became identified with that of ordinary electricity, with the very element, as it were, by which such effects were produced; and the gigantic attempt of Franklin (about seven years afterwards) actually to draw electricity from the clouds, and appropriate it in a similar way to the purpose of experiment, had fully succeeded,—then it was, that these artificial electrical accumulations and discharges acquired a more than ordinary interest, as furnishing us with a valuable means of investigating by minor experiments, the laws and operations of the great discharge in thunderstorms.

The identity of common electricity and lightning, although not fully verified until the year 1752, had nevertheless been long suspected. Mr. Gray, an English electrician, observes (*Phil. Trans.* for 1735), that "the electric fire seems to be of the same nature with that of thunder and lightning,"* and the celebrated Abbé Nollet, in his *Leçons de Physique*, acutely describes many great points of resemblance between them. "If any one (he observes) should take upon him to prove from a well connected comparison of phenomena, that thunder is, in the hands of nature, what electricity is in ours,—that the wonders we exhibit at our pleasure are little imitations of those great effects which inspire us with awe, and that the whole depends upon the same mechanism, if it is to be demonstrated that a cloud prepared by the action of winds, by heat, &c., is an electrized body,—I avow this idea, well supported, would be to me a source of great delight."

At length Franklin in America, and several philosophers in France, conceived the grand thought of bringing the element of lightning out of the atmosphere, by means of pointed conducting bodies; and in the year 1752 electrical sparks were drawn from the clouds. Tired of waiting for the erection of a spire at Philadelphia, on which he proposed to fix a pointed rod of iron, the American philosopher had recourse to a common kite, as affording an immediate and ready access to the region of lightnings. The kite had a pointed wire, and the twine which held it was attached to an insulating cord of silk. A passing shower opportunely wetted the twine, and increased

* Dr. Wall also observes, *Phil. Trans.*, vol. xxvi., that the crackling sound and light produced by the excitation of amber represents in some degree thunder and lightning.

its conducting power,—at the same moment electrical sparks were drawn from a key hung on the extremity of the kite-string.

In the mean time, Dalibard and Delor, both zealous partisans of Franklin, had drawn electrical sparks from the clouds at Paris and in its vicinity, by means of pointed iron rods, forty feet in length, elevated upon some of the highest ground they could find; and thus was verified one of the most interesting and important theories to be found in the history of physics.

Dr. Franklin, in remarking on the similarity between common electricity and lightning, cautions his readers against any degree of disparity of effect as an argument against the identity of these powers. It is no wonder, he says, that the effects of the one so far surpass the other. "If two gun-barrels, when electrified, will strike at two inches distance, and make a loud report, at how great a distance may 10,000 acres of electrified cloud strike, and how loud must be that crack?"

The great points of coincidence between the common electric discharge and lightning may be thus specified:—

Flashes of lightning are frequently waving and crooked, of a zig-zag or forked appearance, sometimes diffuse and colored—the same is true of sparks drawn from the ordinary electrical machine.

Lightning most commonly falls on elevated or pointed objects—the same is true of electricity.

Lightning seizes on the readiest and best line of

transit in its course to the earth—the same is true of the common electrical discharge.

Lightning burns up various kinds of matter—fuses and ignites metallic bodies—the same is true of the electrical discharge.

Lightning rends brittle substances, and scatters various kinds of matter, as if they were acted on by a violent expansive force—such is also the case with electricity.

Lightning impresses on living animals a peculiar nervous shock, and sometimes destroys life—this is also the case with electricity.

Lightning reverses, destroys, or gives magnetic polarity to steel—such is also the result of powerful electrical discharges.

When these coincidences are considered, together with the fact that electricity may be drawn out of the clouds and air, and applied to produce precisely the same effects as those resulting from a common electrical machine, it becomes quite evident that the cause, whatever it be, of ordinary electrical phenomena, is identical with that of lightning; consequently we arrive at the important deduction, that common electricity and lightning are subject to the same laws,—a deduction which cannot be too forcibly insisted on, involving as it does the most valuable practical consequences.

Nature of ordinary Electrical Arrangements producing Artificial Lightning.

The great discovery of the electrical jar, to which

we have adverted (p. 23), involves, in fact, all the conditions of a thunderstorm, the disruptive discharge from the jar being the same in effect as thunder and lightning. This will be immediately perceived by referring to what has been already advanced on this subject (pp. 12, 15), where it may be seen that the conditions there represented are reducible to the separation of two conducting planes, P, N (fig. 1), by an intermediate insulating substance A; one of the conductors, P, being limited, the other, N, of indefinite extent. Now, to complete such a system artificially, we have only to attach two conducting surfaces, P, N (fig. 6), to the opposite sides of a square of glass, A, B, leaving about an inch of

FIG. 6.

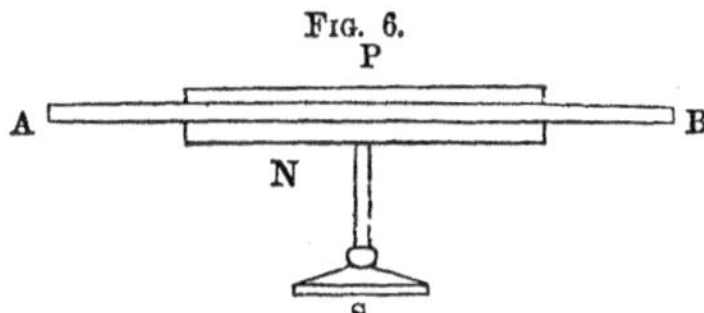

the glass clear and projecting between the two. If such a system be placed on a conducting base, communicating with the earth, it is evident we have a limited and insulated conductor, P, opposed to a conductor, N, of indefinite extent. Directly we charge this system on the insulated surface, P, the two conducting surfaces, P N, become the terminating planes of a great electrical action, and the particles of the glass become polarized by induction (p. 15): hence this system is precisely the same as that represented in fig. 4. The nature of the insulating substance between the planes, does not in any way interfere with the conditions of this arrangement, nor does its thickness, because induction goes on at all distances. Faraday traced it from a small electrified ball in the middle of a room to the walls, twenty-six feet distant.* It takes place, however, with the same constraining force, more readily according as the extent of the intervening insulation is lessened. Hence it is, that with a small thickness of glass we obtain a very intense action, the density and compactness of the glass furnishing a resistance, sufficient to maintain the particles in their polarized condition. This is not the case with a gaseous insulation, such as air, the particles of which soon break down at small distances, under the reactive force of the opposite electrical powers (pp. 15, 19).

It is, however, requisite here to understand, that disruptive discharges from this arrangement are generally obtained by neutralizing the forces through a side circuit of conductors; that is to say, instead of

FIG. 7.

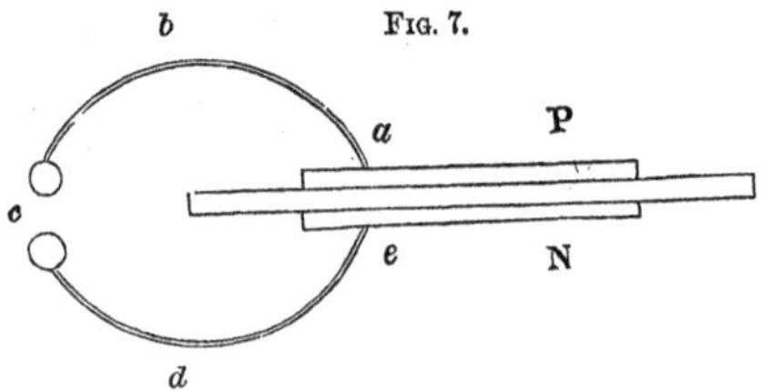

allowing the intermediate glass to become broken down by the force between the conducting planes, P,

* *Researches in Electricity*, p. 411.

N, as supposed in figs. 1 and 4, we discharge the system through a side circuit, *a b c d e* (fig. 7). This, however, is of no consequence to the result of this experiment, because the laws of such discharges, by which the system is reduced to electrical quiescence, remain the same; and any substance exposed to the effects of the discharge in the interval, *c*, would be affected in precisely the same way as if it were in the interval, P, N, immediately between the terminating planes.

Thus, suppose P N (fig. 8), to be the terminating planes of a great electrical disturbance in an interval

FIG. 8.

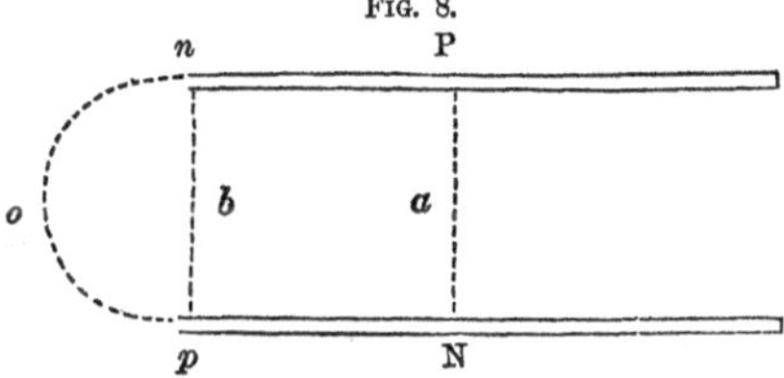

of air. Imagine a conducting path suddenly opened, and the system discharged: it is clear that whether such a path were opened immediately between the planes as at P *a* N, or at the edge of the planes as at *n b p*, the result must be the same. Now, imagine the conducting circuit at the edge of the planes to be curved into the form *n o p*, still this could not possibly affect the law of the discharge in the circuit, —but this last is the case in question. Suppose, further, we had made a disruptive interval in this discharging conductor in any point of it, as *o*, *b*, *a*, still the result of the discharge in such an interval would remain invariable; consequently we may assume any one of the three paths of discharge, P *a* N, *n b p*, *n o p*, to be a casual association of bad and good conductors, as in the case of a building, without in any way affecting the law of the discharge through them. Therefore let the immediate position of the line of discharge be what it may, whether immediately between the planes P, N, or extending without them as at *n o b*, or whether interrupted by a large interval P *a*, *n b*, *n o*, still the laws regulating the neutralization of the opposite electrical forces through such a disjointed circuit must be always the same.

Then, with respect to the immediate mechanical form or arrangement of such a system, that is also a matter of indifference; we may make the system cylindrical if we please, and hence the immediate application of the principle to the Leyden experiment or electrical jar. This piece of electrical apparatus in its improved state, consists of two conducting surfaces P, N (fig. 9), pasted on the opposite sides of a glass jar, a portion of the glass *d d* being left clear and projecting between them. When electricity is communicated to the interior insulated surface P, by means of a rod *a c*, the outer surface N resting on the ground, the whole system becomes charged as in the former case, and may hence be in like manner discharged by means of a curved metallic wire *n b*, and if we connect the charging rods of many such jars, all resting on a common conducting base, we may charge and discharge the whole together, as one great system of enormous power, and produce effects approaching to those of lightning. With the great battery in the Tylerian Museum at Haerlem, which exposed 225 square feet of insulated metallic surface *d*, Van Marum gave polarity to steel bars nine

Fig. 9.

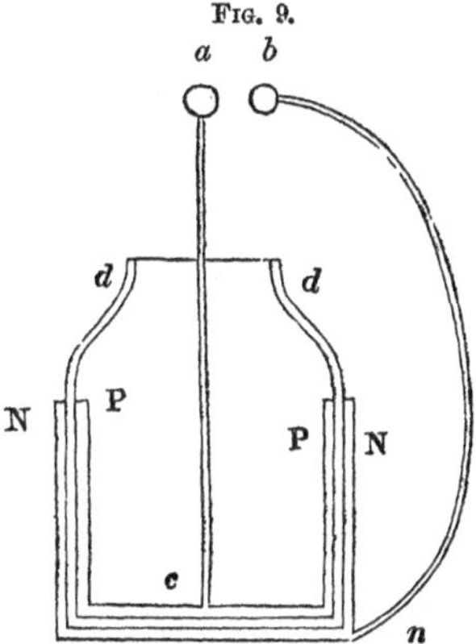

inches long, nearly half an inch wide, and one-twelfth of an inch thick. A piece of box-wood four inches in diameter and four inches in length was rent by it in pieces. It melted readily various metals, and dispersed them in all directions. An iron wire twenty-five feet long, and about $\frac{1}{140}$th of an inch in diameter, fell under the shock, into red hot balls dispersing in all directions. A piece of tin wire eight inches long, and one-eighteenth of an inch in diameter, disappeared in a cloud of blue smoke, throwing down red-hot globules of tin, which repeatedly rebounded from a piece of paper beneath it.* In the course of similar experiments by Mr. Brook, he says, "the report was so very loud, that our ears were stunned, and the flash of light so very great, that my sight was quite confused for a few seconds."

The electrical machine employed by Van Marum consisted of two circular plates of glass, each five feet five inches in diameter: these were set on the same axis, and were rendered electrical by revolving with friction between eight cushions, each about fifteen inches long, and two inches wide. The power of this splendid instrument was such, that bodies at forty feet distance were sensibly influenced; pointed wires became tipped with a star of light at twenty-eight feet distance (p. 19), and a powerful current of brilliant light two feet or more in length, crooked, and darting forth luminous brushes into the air, was obtained by presenting a metallic ball in connection with the earth, to its great conductor. A single spark melted a considerable length of gold-leaf, and fired various kinds of combustibles.

We have thought it not unimportant to notice these results, as having a direct bearing on the great question of the defence of buildings from lightning. For since the accumulation of electricity by artificial means may be carried to an almost indefinite extent, and is equally manageable, whatever may be the extreme limit of force we choose to assign to such accumulation,—it necessarily follows that discharges

* Roz. xxxiii. and *Phil. Mag.*, vol. viii.; Nich. ii. 527.

of atmospheric electricity may be quite as easily directed, by a judicious and scientific arrangement of conducting bodies; such discharges being in fact, nothing more than the same force also resulting from a species of electrical machine, and accumulated in a similar way, by means of an apparatus of a perfectly similar kind. The vapory masses of the clouds, opposed through the intermediate air to the surface of ground or sea, constitute a battery of enormous power. The circumstance of the coatings of the jar being metallic, whilst those in nature consist of water, is a difference of no moment whatever; especially when we consider that the original experiment of the Dutch philosophers, consisted in the electrification of water inclosed in a small phial, from which they obtained so great a shock, as to induce one of them to say that he would not again receive it for the whole kingdom of France.

Various Phenomena of Lightning and Thunder.

The identity of ordinary electrical discharges with the phenomena of thunder and lightning being thus satisfactorily shown, we have now merely to consider some of those modifications of the effect, characteristic of these great natural operations. In the first place, it is to be observed, that when the discharge takes place very close to the observer, the effect is a brilliant vivid light of momentary duration, intolerable to the eye, and attended by a terrific and sudden whizzing crash, as if ten thousand porcelain jars had fallen on a stone pavement, and were smashed in pieces.

When, however, some considerable distance is interposed, the light is more tolerable, and precedes the crash by a sensible time; in this case the noise begins to soften down into a sort of reverberating roar; at still greater distances the reverberations are taken up, and bandied about between the irregular forms of the distant clouds and the surface of the earth, producing what has been termed, in common language, peals of thunder. A similar effect ensues on the earth's surface, during the discharge of cannon, where surrounding objects present irregular sources of reverberation: on the sea, where so few obstacles to the diffusion of sound exist, distant thunder regularly dies away in a sort of sullen silence. The distance of the point of discharge, may be estimated by the time which elapses between the flash of lightning and the thunder; since for small distances, the progress of light may be taken as instantaneous: sound, on the contrary, has a more sensible duration, being propagated through the air, at the rate of eleven hundred feet in a second. It may be here remarked, that an essential distinction exists between the *light* of lightning, for which, as Franklin observes, we want an appropriate term, and the presence of the electrical agency itself.

Arago divides the phenomena of lightning into three classes. In the first he places those luminous discharges characterized by a long streak of light, very thin, and well defined at the edges: they are not always white, but are sometimes of a violet or purple hue; they do not move in a straight line, but have a deviating track of a zig-zag form. They frequently divide in striking terrestrial objects, into two or more distinct streams, but invariably proceed from a single point. The Abbé Richard witnessed a discharge of this kind descend from a cloud, and divide upon two separate objects on coming near the earth.* We have instances, in the damage done to our shipping, of the trifurcation of lightning, in which the three masts of a ship have all been struck by the same discharge. This result ensued in His Majesty's ship *Implacable*, under the command of Sir George Cockburn, in July, 1810, near the Isle of Wight. The fore and mizzen topgallant-masts were shivered, and traces of the discharge were left on the main-mast.

Under the second class, Arago has placed those luminous effects not having any apparent depth, but expanding over a vast surface: they are frequently colored red, blue, and violet; they have not the activity of the former class, and are generally confined to the edges of the cloud from which they appear to proceed.

The third class comprises those more concentrated masses of light, which he has termed globular lightning. The long zig-zag and expanded flashes, exist but for a moment, but these seem to endure for many seconds: they appear to occupy time, and to have a progressive motion.

It is more than probable, that many of these

* *Histoire Naturelle de l'Air et des Météores.*

phenomena are at least reducible to the common progress of the disruptive discharge, modified by the quantity of passing electricity, the density and condition of the air, and the brilliancy of the attendant light. When the state of the atmosphere is such, that a moderately intense discharge can proceed in an occasionally deviating zig-zag line, the great nucleus, or head of the discharge, becomes drawn out as it were, into a line of light visible through the whole track; and if the discharge divides on approaching a terrestrial object, we have what sailors call forked lightning. If it does not divide, but exhibits a long rippling line, with but little deviation, then they call it chain lightning. What sailors term sheet lightning, is the light of a vivid discharge reflected from the surfaces of distant clouds, the spark itself being concealed by a dense intermediate mass of cloud, behind which the discharge has taken place. In this way an extensive range of cloud may appear in a blaze of light, producing a truly sublime effect. The appearance termed globular lightning, may be the result of similar discharges; it is no doubt always attended by a diffusely luminous track, this may, however, be completely eclipsed in the mind of the observer, by the great concentration and density of the discharge, in the points immediately through which it continues to force its way, and where the condensation of the air immediately before it is often extremely great. It is this intensely illuminated point which gives the notion of globular discharge; and it is clear, from the circumference of air which may become illuminated, the apparent diameter will be often great. Mr. Hearder, of Plymouth, once witnessed a discharge of lightning of this kind on the Dartmoor hills, very near him. Several vivid flashes had occurred, before the mass of clouds approached the hill on which he was standing: before he had time to retreat from his dangerous position, a tremendous crash and explosion burst close to him. To use his own words, "the spark had the appearance of a nucleus of intensely ignited matter, followed by a flood of light; it struck the path near me, and dashed with fearful brilliancy down its whole length, to a rivulet at the foot of the hill, where it terminated."

Appearances termed Fire-Balls.

A great deal has been said relative to these appearances, and some doubts have been entertained of their real existence as mere balls of electrical light. Nevertheless the evidence of the existence of a form of disruptive discharge, faithfuly conveying to the observer such an impression, is beyond question. A curious instance is given by Mr. Chalmers whilst on board the *Montague*, of seventy-four guns, bearing the flag of Admiral Chambers. In the account read at the Royal Society,* he states that "November 4th, 1749, whilst taking an observation on the quarterdeck, one of the quartermasters requested him to look to windward; upon which he

* *Phil. Trans.*, vol. xlvi., p. 366.

observed a large ball of blue fire rolling along on the surface of the water, as big as a mill-stone, at about three miles distance. Before they could raise the main-tack, the ball had reached within forty yards of the main-chains, when it rose perpendicularly with a fearful explosion, and shattered the main-topmast in pieces." In an account of the fatal effects of lightning, in June, 1826, on the Malvern Hills, when two young ladies were struck dead, it is stated that the electric discharge "appeared as a mass of fire rolling along the hill towards the building in which the party had taken shelter."*

The great number of accounts of such appearances, and the remarkable coincidences in them all, extending as they do through nearly a whole century, and consequently given by observers in no way connected with each other, leave not the least doubt of their existence. M. Deslandes transmitted to the Academy of Science in Paris an account of a terrible thunderstorm in Brittany, in April 1718, which completely destroyed a church near Brest. In this account it is stated that the damage was done by three large globes of fire of three feet and a half in diameter, which fell at once on the spire.†

It is by no means easy to explain these appearances on the principles applicable to the ordinary electric spark: the amazing rapidity with which this proceeds, and the momentary duration of the light

* *Loyd's Evening Post.*

† *Annuaire* pour 1838, p. 259.

(p. 8), renders it almost a matter of impossibility that the discharge should appear under the form of a ball of fire; it would be a transient line of light: we must look, therefore, to some other source for an explanation of these appearances.

Now it is not improbable, that in many cases in which distinct balls of fire of sensible duration have been perceived, the appearance has resulted from the species of brush or glow discharge already described (p. 19), and which may often precede the main shock: the ball of fire, observed by M. Toscan at the Botanic Gardens in Paris, was evidently a result of this kind. In short, it is not difficult to conceive, that before a discharge of the whole system takes place, that is to say, before the constrained condition of the dielectric particles of air intermediate between the clouds and earth (p. 15) becomes as it were overturned, the particles nearest one of the terminating planes, or other bodies situate on them, may begin to discharge upon the succeeding particles, and make an effort to restore the neutral condition of the system by a gradual process. Such was doubtless the case in the instances given by M. Deslandes and M. Toscan.

If therefore we conceive the discharging particles to have progressive motion from any cause, then we shall immediately obtain such a result as that observed by Mr. Chalmers on board the *Montague* (p. 38), in which a large ball of blue fire was observed rolling on the surface of the water, towards the ship from *to windward.* This was evidently a sort of glow discharge, or St. Helmo's fire, produced by some of the polarized atmospheric particles yielding up their electricity to the surface of the water, much in the same way, as, in the appearance observed by M. Toscan, the stationary cloud did on the land. The clouds, however, were here in rapid motion, the ship at the time being under topsails and courses only, in consequence of the strength of the wind: the discharging particles, therefore, had motion towards the ship, the rate of which appears, from the account to correspond with the velocity of the breeze. On nearing the ship, the point of discharge became transferred to the head of the mast; and the striking distance being thus diminished, the whole system returned to its normal state (p. 12), that is to say, a disruptive discharge ensued between the sea and the clouds (p. 15), producing the usual phenomena of thunder and lightning, termed by the observers, the "rising of the ball through the mast of the ship." The fatal occurrence on the Malvern Hills (p. 39) is another instance of the same kind. A similar effect is described in the *Phil. Trans.* for 1773, in which a ball of light appeared in the parlor of a house struck by lightning at Steeple Ashton. The ball is described as being of "the size of a sixpenny loaf, and surrounded with a dark smoke," and is said "to have burst with a loud noise." This too was evidently a species of brush or glow discharge (p. 21), preceding the stroke of lightning which damaged the house.

It is therefore highly probable, that all these appearances so decidedly marked as concentrated balls of fire, are produced by the glow or brush discharge producing a St. Helmo's fire in a given point or points of the charged system (p. 15), previously to the more general and rapid union of the electrical forces; whilst the greater number of discharges described as globular lightning, are, as already observed, most probably nothing more than a vivid and dense electrical spark in the act of breaking through the air,—which, coming suddenly on the eye, and again vanishing in an extremely small portion of time, has been designated a ball of light. Thus in a thunderstorm which damaged a house at Eastbourne, in Sussex, in September 1781, balls of fire were said to dart from the clouds into the sea. These were evidently common electrical sparks seen at a distance; for when the lightning struck the house, "multitudes saw the meteor dart in a right line over their heads, and all agreed that the form and flame were exactly like that of an immense sky-rocket."*

Sulphurous Odor of the Electric Discharge.

There is one circumstance noticed by the celebrated Italian philosopher, Beccaria, which must not be lost sight of, as having doubtless great influence over these appearances, viz., the tendency of the electrical discharge to drag into its path light conducting substances, which can facilitate its progress,

* *Phil. Trans.* for 1781, p. 42.

and by which it is enabled to strike through distances considerably greater than would otherwise be traversed. Thus traces of smoke, free vapor, or any other conducting matter floating in the air, will frequently determine the course of lightning, and not only determine it as to direction, but greatly modify its appearance. A heated or whirling column of air, such as is sometimes seen to arise even in a tranquil state of the weather, would produce a similar effect through its interior and rarefied portion; and there is little doubt that conducting matter, when dragged into the path of lightning, would be intensely heated and decomposed. Beccaria once received an electric shock through the fumes of nitric acid, which became concentrated and driven into his thumb producing a small round hole; and Priestley found that a discharge could be produced, by the dispersion of a drop of water which hung on a brass rod communicating with the inside of his battery.

The transfer and ignition of ponderable matter through the track of electrical discharge, may be adduced to explain, in some degree, the suffocating sulphurous odor so frequently observed at the time of heavy strokes of lightning: on ship-board more especially, when great damage has arisen, and the electrical discharge has exploded below decks, this sulphurous smell is described as quite suffocating. In the case of the *Montague*, just cited (p. 38), it is said of this odor, that "the ship seemed to be nothing but sulphur." From whence this arises is still an interesting problem in physics. There are many facts, which favor the idea of various kinds of matter being dragged and transported into the track of the electrical discharge, either immediately from the body of the earth, or from the atmosphere in which they are often found; and it is not impossible in this way to explain those apparently solid balls of fire termed more especially meteors; that vapors of various kinds may greatly modify and direct disruptive discharge, is unquestionable, and hence give rise to those long, truncated appearances of flame frequently observed in discharges of lightning. It would be trespassing on the limits of this work, to enter at length upon the theory of meteors, or upon those chemical views which some able philosophers have entertained, of the nature of the odor emitted by the electrical discharge; it may perhaps be sufficient for our present purpose to keep it in view, without an elaborate detail of its possible causes.*

Artificial Disruptive Discharges.

The luminous appearances observable in the great and terrible discharges of lightning, may be completely obtained by artificial means, giving rise to

* Mr. Benjamin Cook, F. R. S., states, that after a night of vivid lightning, with thunder, an oblong ball, of a bright yellow color, and frosted over with fine yellow crystals, was found in a meadow far from any house, and in a perfectly undisturbed surface of ground. The ball appeared quite fresh. The crystals were easily displaced, and the matter of the ball was principally sulphur. It burned with mild sulphurous flames.—*Phil. Trans.*, vol. xl.

experiments of a highly instructive kind. The conditions which modify the extent and appearance of the electrical discharge, produced artificially, are the form and extent of the conductors—between which the disturbance has taken place, the quantity of accumulated electricity, the intensity of the charge, and the nature and density of the medium through which it forces its way. Between round and even surfaces, of considerable extent as compared with the amount of electricity accumulated, the sparks, under common states of the air, are short and dense, approaching in appearance globular lightning: and this is true in respect of electricity passing between any two parallel surfaces, and is even applicable to the conditions of the discharge of the electrical jar. The opposed conductors P N (fig. 7), so influence the form, appearance, and dimensions of the spark, that we cannot obtain under common circumstances, through the neutralizing circuit *a b c d e*, a more extensive discharge than could take place, supposing it to have occurred immediately between P N, the terminating planes themselves. Short dense discharges are in each case produced, approaching in appearance to many of those in nature, called by sailors, fireballs.

By changing the disposition and form of the conductors, we obtain longer and more diffuse sparks, of a zig-zag and waving character, which frequently bifurcate, and otherwise divide, producing appearances similar to those termed by mariners, forked and chain lightning. All this greatly depends on the activity of the charge, which again varies with the extent of surface upon which it passes; the activity of electricity disposed on surfaces varying in dimensions, being in an inverse duplicate ratio of the surface, the quantity being constant;* that is to say, a given quantity of electricity collected on a double extent of conducting surface, has only one-fourth the activity—on a treble extent only one-ninth—and so on. Hence an electrical disturbance which, between terminating planes of large dimensions, would be comparatively quiescent, becomes active and unruly between planes of much less extent. When large quantities of electricity, therefore, press upon small surfaces, the spark is elongated and spiteful in its character; and if these be indefinitely reduced to mere points, the discharge is narrowed into a sort of stream, causing a rapid escape of the electricity under such an attenuated form, as to produce a comparatively tranquil and gradual discharge (p. 19). It is, as observed by Faraday, when treating of this curious action of pointed conductors, at the extremity of a point, that the intensity necessary to charge the air is first acquired; from thence the particles recede. At the same time, the point, having become the origin of an active mechanical force, does, by the very act of causing that force, namely, by discharge, prevent any other part of the conducting body from which it projects, from acquiring the same condition, and thus preserves its own predominance. In this way

* *Phil. Trans.* for 1834, p. 221.

pointed conductors operate in discharging large accumulations at considerable distances, under the form of stream, brush, or glow, and so parry the violent concentrated explosion commonly attendant on them. This result ensues whether the pointed conductor be affixed to the charged body or not—the opposite electrical state being always produced in every case of discharge. Thus, if we present a pointed metallic body to the conductor of the machine, in the act of throwing off dense and brilliant sparks, such sparks can no longer be obtained (p. 11)—the electric matter being silently drawn off by the point.

Brush discharge exhibits a great variety of character in different media; its color, form, and sound, being all greatly modified, according as it takes place on a positive or negative surface. Nitrogen gas, which enters in the proportion of four-fifths into the composition of the atmosphere, has the greatest power of originating this kind of discharge. The brushes in this gas, are always fine in form, light, and color; and in nitrogen rarefied by the air-pump the effects are still more striking.

Brush discharge in air from a positive point (p. 15) is frequently diffuse and spreading, producing the appearance called by sailors comazants, or St. Helmo's fires; from a negative point (p. 15) it has often the character of a luminous star, exhibiting the appearances mentioned by Pliny and other ancient writers (p. 21).

When the air in contact with a metallic conductor is rapidly charging, the end of the conductor will often become covered with a glow of lambent light, producing a peculiarly beautiful appearance; this is greatly increased either by decreasing the atmospheric pressure, or by augmenting the electrical force. Faraday produced on a brass ball within an exhausted receiver, a glow of light over an area of two inches. The glow came over the ball, and gradually increased in brightness until it was at last very luminous, and stood up like a low flame of half an inch or more in length,* being analogous to one of the natural phenomena already mentioned (p. 21).

When the discharge is assisted by traces of conducting matter, it will traverse very considerable distances. Thus a trace of sulphuric acid, or small particles of charcoal, or metallic dust, dispersed over a strip of glass, will enable a battery to produce a brilliant and intensely luminous discharge, over a considerable distance. A trace of smoke will in like manner facilitate the progress of the explosion. When the intermediate air is highly rarefied in a tube of glass, a jar may be discharged through it to the extent of several feet, sometimes in one dense mass, in others producing bifurcations and various colored streams.

In the vacuum of a well-boiled barometer, the electrical light is frequently of a beautiful green

* *Experimental Researches*, p. 47.

color, and in media of different kinds varying in density, the color of the spark is altogether changed. Thus in carbonic acid gas it is white and vivid, in hydrogén gas it is red and faint. All this again becomes modified by the quantity of electricity, and by the kind and form of the conductors from which it takes place. Considering, therefore, all these circumstances, it is not at all surprising that we find lightning assuming so great a variety of appearance.

Further Observations on Thunder Clouds.

Although the disruptive discharge of thunderstorms, commonly proceeds at once through the air intermediate between the charged clouds and the earth, yet other more complicated discharges have been supposed to occur, in consequence of electrical disturbances between distinct and distant portions of the atmosphere, in which the surface of the earth becomes involved as a line of discharge between them. The Italian philosopher, Beccaria, entertained opinions of this kind; he seemed to consider it impossible that any cloud or collection of clouds, should contain the great quantity of electricity observed in thunderstorms, so as either to discharge or receive it. He states that, during the progress of a storm, although the lightning frequently struck the earth, yet the clouds were the next moment ready to make a still greater discharge; and hence he concludes that "the electrical matter is continually darting from the clouds in one place, at the same time that it is discharged from the earth in another." The knowledge, however, we now possess, of the nature and extent of electrical action, renders it quite unnecessary to resort to such hypothetical views, in order to explain this phenomenon. The immense absorption and evolution of electricity attendant on chemical and other changes in common matter, is quite sufficient to account for the apparently great quantity of electricity active in thunderstorms. Faraday has shown by strong experimental evidence, that the quantity of electricity holding the elements of a single grain of water in chemical combination, is equal to that discharged in an ordinary flash of lightning, and would, if discharged under the form of a current through a wire of platinum about $\frac{1}{104}$ of an inch in diameter, keep it red-hot in the air, for nearly four minutes.* The simple view, therefore, which we have taken of the electrical conditions of a thunderstorm, is in no way embarrassed by any difficulty arising out of the great quantity of electricity liable to be discharged. Besides, it is not clear that the quantity is so great in relation to conducting bodies, as might at first be supposed. It is to be recollected, that we often judge of the quantity of electricity present, by very deceptive effects,—as by the light of the spark, the noise and expansive force of the discharge, and by the damage done to imperfect conducting matter. Now, we have seen (p. 31) that comparatively small

* *Experimental Researches in Electricity*, p. 250.

quantities of electricity will produce intense effects of this kind; and it is doubtful whether any quantity of electricity ever discharged in a single flash of lightning has been sufficient to melt a copper rod a foot in length and three-fourths of an inch in diameter.

The general condition of a thunderstorm is, as already observed, (p. 5), the charging and discharging of a stratum of air intermediate between the masses of cloud and the earth, or otherwise intermediate between two masses of clouds in opposite electric states; the source of the charge being the evolution of electricity in consequence of certain physical changes in the state and condition of the atmosphere. Discharges of lightning produced by this state of things, may arise during the formation or presence of clouds in a given place, or during their formation and motion through the air, by which a large stratum of polarized particles is swept along over the earth's surface; or they may arise from the motion of an upper current of cloud over a large track of atmosphere, which has from any previous train of circumstances, become polarized; or otherwise, from the operation of successive superimposed strata of air and clouds, reaching to the surface of the earth; or otherwise, from the operation of distant and distinct portions of the atmosphere, oppositely charged, and which may hence discharge into each other, under a great variety of conditions.

Electrical Discharges.

Thunderstorms arising out of a rapid formation of vapor, and in a limited portion of the air, as illustrated in fig. 1, (p. 13,) have been well described by Beccaria. "The first appearance of a thunder-storm," he says, "generally happens when there is little or no wind; there is one dense cloud or more, increasing very fast in size, and rising into the higher regions of the air. The lower surface is black, and nearly level, but the upper is finely arched, and well-defined. Many of these clouds seem piled one over another, all arched in the same way, but they keep continually uniting, swelling, and extending their arches. At the time of the rising of this cloud, the atmosphere is generally full of a great number of separate clouds of whimsical and irregular shapes, and apparently motionless. All these upon the appearance of the thunder cloud draw towards it, become more uniform in their shape, and at length form with it one common mass. Sometimes the thunder cloud will swell very fast without the conjunction of such clouds, and when it is grown to a great size, its lower surface is frequently ragged, and swells into large protuberances which bend uniformly toward the earth; sometimes one whole side of the cloud has an inclination toward the earth. When the eye is under the thunder cloud, it is at last seen to darken fearfully, and a number of small clouds, the origin of which is never detected, drive about it in uncertain directions. Rain and hail about this time fall in abundance. During the swelling and extension of the cloud over a large tract of country, lightning darts through its mass, and at length strikes toward the earth in opposite places; the longer the lightning continues, the rarer the cloud becomes, till at length it breaks up in different places, and shows a clear sky."*

Captain Ward, R. N., gives the following interesting account of the phenomena observed by him during a thunderstorm in the Bay of Honduras in the West Indies, whilst he was in command of his Majesty's ship *Pelican*, in the autumn of the year 1806. "The night was nearly calm, and the heat oppressive; heavy black clouds intensely charged with the electric fluid, overspread the earth, and about midnight, after a little whirl of wind, began to approach it. A discharge of lightning of the most splendid, and at the same time most awful character, speedily ensued. The electric fluid seemed to pour down upon the earth and sea in repeated streams, occasionally illuminating every thing about us with a brilliancy surpassing noon-day, but leaving us at the next instant in pitchy darkness. This fearful display, attended by roaring peals of thunder, lasted about an hour, during which one of the discharges fell on our main-royal mast-head, shivered it, together with the top-gallant mast and topmast in atoms, scattering the fragments to an immense

* *Lettere dell' Elettrismo*, p. 151 to 167.

distance, so that not a piece of any size could be found. The discharge continued its course with damage along the mainmast in an irregular spiral form down to the very heel and step of the mast, where it disappeared."

One of the most awful accounts, however, of a thunderstorm at sea is that given by an intelligent observer, present as a passenger in the splendid American packet-ship *New-York*, which was struck and damaged by lightning in the Gulf-stream, April 19th, 1827, in her passage from New-York to Liverpool. "About half-past five in the morning, being in our berths, we were roused by a sound like the report of heavy cannon close to our ears. In a moment we were all out. From the deck the word was quickly passed that the ship had been struck by lightning, and was on fire. Every one ran on deck; there, all the elements were in violent commotion: it had been broad day, but so dark, so dense, and so close upon us were the clouds, that they produced almost the obscurity of night. There was just sufficient light to give a bold relief to every object in the appalling scene; the rain poured down in torrents, mingled with hailstones as large as filberts; these lay upon the deck nearly an inch thick; overhead blazed the lightning on all sides, accompanied by simultaneous reports; the sea ran mountains high, and the ship was tossed rapidly from one sea to another. One appearance was peculiarly remarkable: the temperature of the water was 74° of Fahrenheit, whilst that of the atmosphere was only 48°. This caused, by evaporation and condensation, immense clouds of vapor, which ascending in columns all around us, exhibited the appearance of innumerable pillars supporting a massive canopy of clouds. In all directions might be seen water-spouts, which rising fearfully to the clouds, seemed actually to present to the eye a combination of all the elements for the destruction of every thing on the face of the deep." These accounts afford highly instructive examples of the spontaneous evolution of electricity in the atmosphere, giving rise to a vast electrical disturbance, and subsequent disruptive discharges (p. 15).

The altitude of the masses of cloud, forming the upper terminating plane of the electrified system, does not appear to be so considerable as their horizontal dimensions, which not unfrequently extend over a large tract of country, producing almost simultaneous discharges in various places. Admiral Ross states, that the storm which shivered the masts of the *Désirée* in Port Antonio, Jamaica, in the autumn of 1803, was witnessed by an observer some short distance up the adjacent hill. It appeared to take place close under him, during a fine clear, starlight evening overhead.

On the night of the 14th of April, 1718, a thunderstorm occupied the coast of Brittany between Landerneau and St. Pol de Leon, and damaged no less than twenty-four church towers.* In 1774 a

* *Annuaire* pour 1838, p. 479.

severe thunderstorm spread itself over London. The lightning damaged St. Peter's church considerably, and at the same time several other discharges occurred in various places far distant from each other. A Dutch ship in the river off the Tower was struck, also the obelisk in St. George's fields, Southwark, together with a chimney at Lambeth, and a house at Vauxhall.* On the 11th January, 1815, another thunderstorm occupied no less a space than that contained between the North Sea and the Rhenish provinces, and severely damaged twelve church towers in various parts of this extensive tract.†

The electrical disturbance is sometimes so very rapidly progressive, that repeated discharges are observed to occur in the same place, in quick succession. The church and buildings of the abbey of Nôtre Dame, in the town of Ham, in France, was, during the night of the 25th April, 1760, struck three times in the short interval of twenty minutes, and the whole burnt to the ground.‡ His Majesty's ship *Hyacinth* had first her fore-topmast, then her main-topmast rent in pieces by two discharges which followed close upon each other.§

His Majesty's ship *Madagascar*, in coming to an anchor in the Corfu Channel, in January, 1829, was struck by lightning no less than five times within two hours; the sails were set on fire, and other

* *Phil. Trans.*, vol. lxiv. for 1774.
† *Annuaire* pour 1838, p. 481.
‡ Idem, p. 482.
§ *Report of Commission*, p. 75.

damage done. His Majesty's ship *Ætna* was in the same storm, and not far distant; she experienced repeated discharges: "the descent of the electric fluid was frequent and at very short intervals." *

His Majesty's frigate *Clorinde* was struck and damaged by lightning, on the coast of Ceylon, in the spring of the year 1813. The following is a very clear and circumstantial account of the phenomena, by Captain Briggs, R. N., who commanded the ship. "*The weather was moderate.* About three in the afternoon we observed a dark cloud approaching the ship from the *windward* quarter: this induced me to clew up the topsails. About an hour afterwards, the ship was struck by lightning: the cloud we had observed, was charged with electricity, and had burst on the ship. The mainmast was shivered in pieces; only a wreck remained. Three men were killed, and many hurt."

Now it is clear, that in this instance, the disruptive discharge was caused by the progressive motion of a charged cloud, driven by an upper current, upon a comparatively tranquil air, but possibly in a polarized state, sweeping along with it a portion of charged atmosphere, and accumulating forces, sufficient to make it approach the earth, within a distance at which the forces could neutralize through the intermediate stratum.

The following is a similar instance, related by Captain Haydon, R. N., in which the whole atmosphere and cloud travelled together in the direction

* *Report of Commission*, p. 87.

of the wind. "His Majesty's ship *Cambrian*, off Plymouth, February 22, 1799, strong gales and squally; observed a tremendous squall coming down upon us; turned the hands up to clew up the close-reefed topsails. Whilst they were so employed, a ball of fire struck the topmast-head, killed two men and wounded many others. The number taken below amounted to about twenty."

The case of His Majesty's ship *Topaze*, struck by lightning in the West Indies, in July, 1802, is another remarkable instance of this source of disruptive discharge. Captain H. Edwards, R. N., who was in the ship at the time, says, "When off the west end of St. Domingo, about two or three leagues from the shore, we were becalmed. About midnight a light breeze came off the land, bearing a dark isolated cloud; the cloud began to discharge its lightning within an apparently short distance of the ship, and after five or six vividly forked flashes, struck our mizzen royal-mast, and passed down the mizzen-mast, shivering and rending the spars in its course."

It appears that the light breeze from the shore enabled them to get the ship's head the right way, so as to lay her with her stern to the shore: hence the mizzen-mast was the mast first acted on by the cloud.

A great variety of instances might be quoted, in confirmation of disruptive discharges being produced on the principles already explained (p. 12): they all differ from the state of things observable in more stationary thunderstorms (p. 52) in this, that whilst in such thunderstorms, there is often a rapid, and continuous series of discharges produced by the spontaneous evolution of electricity in one place: we trace in the progress of highly electrified clouds, deliberate discharges of a passing kind, few in number, in some instances not extending beyond one or two at the furthest.

Electrical disturbances, involving similar conditions, but of a more complicated character, sometimes proceed with continued destructive effects over a long tract of country, the atmosphere appearing to assume, during the progress of the masses of electrified cloud, an intensely charged state. Such storms have been observed to pass from the southern shores of England to the north of Scotland and Ireland. A thunderstorm of this kind occurred in July, 1827. It began on the south-west coast of Devonshire on Sunday evening, reached Cheltenham the same night, and Glasgow the next morning, the atmosphere throughout this extent appearing to undergo a rapid and progressive change.*

Ascending Stroke.

Sometimes the thunderbolt passes from the earth to the clouds, and in this case it is called by some philosophers the "ascending stroke," by others "the returning stroke." Facts are not wanting to indicate the progress of electricity upward. The Marquis Maffei was the first who observed this curious phe-

* Provincial and London Journals.

nomenon. He distinctly saw, during a storm, the lightning issue from the ground with a loud noise. The Abbe Lioni and M. Segnier of Nismes, saw the lightning rise in the form of flame six feet high, followed by a loud noise.

One of the most interesting cases of the ascending stroke has been recorded by John Williams, Esq. It took place upon the hills above the village of Great Malvern, on the 1st July, 1826. A party had taken refuge from the storm in a circular building roofed with sheet iron, and one of the ladies on entering the hut expressed her alarm lest the lightning should be attracted by the iron roof. They had scarcely entered their retreat, and were about to partake of some refreshment, when a violent storm of thunder and lightning came on from the west. About forty-five minutes past two, a gentleman who stood at the eastern entrance, saw a ball of fire which seemed to him moving on the surface of the ground. It instantly entered the hut, forcing him several paces forward from the doorway. On his recovering from the shock, he found his sisters on the floor of the hut, fainting, as he imagined, from terror. Two of the ladies had died instantly; another lady, and the rest of the party, were much injured. The explosion which followed the flash of lightning, was said, by the inhabitants of the village, to have been terrific. Mr. Williams, who immediately examined the hut, found a large crack in the west side of the building, which passed upward from near the ground to the frame of a small window, above which the iron roof was a little indented. Mr. Williams conceived it to be quite clear, from the place of the fragments of stone and other appearances, that the clouds were negatively electrified during this storm.*

A very curious instance of the ascending stroke is related by G. F. Richter, in his work on thunder. He informs us that in the cellar belonging to the Benedictine monks of Fontigno, while the servants were employed in pouring into a cask some wine which had been just boiled, a fine light flame appeared round the funnel, and they had scarcely finished their operations, when a noise like thunder was heard; the cellar was instantly filled with fire; the cask was burst open, although hooped with iron, the staves were thrown with prodigious violence against the wall, and, on examination, a hole of three inches diameter was found in the bottom of the cask.†

On the 24th of February, 1774, lightning struck the steeple of the village of Rouvroi, to the north-west of Arras. A pavement composed of large blue stones, which was laid under the steeple was violently raised upward.

In the summer of 1787 lightning struck two persons who had taken refuge under a tree near the village of Tacon, in Beaujalois. Their hair was *driven upward and found upon the top of the tree.* A ring of iron which was upon the shoe of one of these persons was found afterwards *suspended on one of the upper branches.*

* *Encyclopædia Britannia*, vol. 8, p. 619.

† *London Encyclopædica*, vol. 8, p. 59.

On the 29th of August, 1808, lightning struck a small building near the hospital of Salpétrière in Paris. A laborer who was in it was killed, and after the event the pieces of his hat were found incrusted on the ceiling of the room.

When trees have been barked by lightning, it frequently happens that the bark is stripped from the base *upward* to a certain height, and the upper part of the tree is untouched. This occurred with several trees in the Champs Elysées, at Paris, in a storm which took place in June, 1778.

The leaves of trees which have been struck by lightning often exhibit the effects of heat on their lower surfaces, but not at all on their superior surfaces.

Among the numerous manifestations of the discharge of electric matter from the surface of the earth, one of the most circumstantial and authentic is due to Brydone, who, being on the spot where the occurrences took place, was in part witness to them, and collected the particulars from other eye-witnesses with scrupulous care.

On the 10th July 1785, a storm broke out between noon and one o'clock, in the neighborhood of Coldstream. During its continuance, there occurred in the surrounding country several remarkable accidents.

A woman who was cutting grass on the banks of the *Tweed*, was suddenly thrown down without any apparent cause. She called her companions immediately to her aid, and told them that she received a sudden and violent blow on the soles of her feet, but whence it proceeded she could not tell. At the moment this happened there was neither thunder nor lightning.

A shepherd attached to a farm called Lennel Hill, saw a sheep suddenly fall, which the moment before appeared in perfect health. He ran to raise it from the ground, and found it stiff dead. The storm was then approaching, but distant.

Two coal-wagons, driven by two boys, seated on the benches in front of them, had just crossed the *Tweed*, and were in the act of ascending a hill on the banks of the river, when a loud explosion was heard like the report of several guns fired nearly together, and unattended by any rolling or continued sound like that which usually accompanies thunder. At the moment of this explosion the boy who drove the second wagon saw the foremost wagon with the two horses and driver suddenly fall to the ground, the coal being scattered about in all directions. On examination, the driver and horses were found to be stiff dead. The coal which was dispersed, had the appearance of having been for some time in the fire. At the points where the tires of the wheels rested at the time of the explosion, the ground was found to be pierced by two circular holes, which being examined by *Brydone* half an hour after the occurrence, emitted a strong odor resembling that of ether. The tires of the wheels showed evident marks of fusion at the points which were in contact with the road at the moment of the explosion, and at no other part.

The hair was singed on the legs and under the bellies of the horses, and by a careful examination of the marks left in the dust of the road where they fell, it was apparent that they must have been struck suddenly stone dead, so that no life remained when they touched the ground. Had there been any convulsive struggle, the marks would have been visible. The body of the driver was scorched in different places, and his dress, shirt, and particularly his hat, were reduced to rags. A strong odor proceeded from them.

All the witnesses of this occurrence agreed, that no luminous appearance whatever attended it. The driver of the second wagon was conversing with his comrade, and was looking toward him at the moment he was struck down, being at about twenty yards behind him, but saw no light. A shepherd standing in an adjacent field, told Mr. Brydone that he had his eye on the wagon at the very instant of the explosion, but he saw no light. He saw a vortex of dust arise at the place of the explosion, but unaccompanied by any luminous appearance. Finally, Mr. Brydone himself at the moment of the event was standing at an open window, with a watch in his hand, explaining to the persons around him the method of calculating the distance of the lightning by observing the interval between the flash and the thunder, and he heard the explosion, but perceived no light.*

Professor Dewey, D. D., of Rochester University,

* *Dr. Lardner's Lectures on Science and Art, Vol. II., p.* 72.

related to the writer some few months since, that during his connection with Williamstown College, Mass., a church in South Williamstown was struck by lightning. The house was carefully examined by himself after it was struck, when he saw leaves of flowers that had grown by the walls of the church, lodged in the cobwebs up under the eaves.

Some time last summer Mr. Platt's house, Deep River, Connecticut, was struck by lightning. After the accident, the house was carefully examined by myself and many others. It was evidently an instance of the "ascending stroke." The front part of the house, including the entire length of the wing attached, was traversed by the lightning, leaving marks of terrific violence wholly unaccountable, unless done by an upward force.

We have multiplied the number of instances under this head, for two reasons: First, because so many of those little read in electrical science utterly disbelieve the existence of an upward stroke, and even laugh at the idea as absurd and whimsical. Secondly, because an intelligent belief in an upward stroke has an important relation to the application of lightning conductors for the protection of buildings, as we shall presently see.

Various electrical phenomena, of a very interesting kind, have been observed by travellers, when ascending lofty mountains. In 1767, M. M. Saussure, Pictet, and Jallabert, when on the top of Mount Breven, received small electric shocks at their finger-ends, by stretching out their arms, and a whistling noise even accompanied them. The gold button on M. Saussure's hat yielded distinct sparks. In 1814, a party of Englishmen experienced similar effects on Mount Ætna, during a storm of thunder and lightning, accompanied by a fall of snow. One of the party felt his hair moving, and upon raising his hand to his head, a buzzing sound issued from his fingers. The rest of the party experienced the same sensations, and by moving their hands and fingers they produced a variety of musical sounds, audible at the distance of forty feet. On the 27th of June, 1825, Dr. Hooker and a party of botanists witnessed effects like those described, during a fall of snow on Ben-Nevis, when there was no thunderstorm. The snow fell very heavily for nearly two hours. Soon after it began, a hissing sound was heard every where around them, and continued about an hour and a half. It seemed to proceed from every point in the vicinity; and on arriving at the cairn on the summit of the mountain, they could almost determine the stones from which the electricity issued. The hair of several of the party exhibited, when touched, the usual electrical phenomena.*

* *Encyclopædia Britannica*, vol. viii. p. 620.

SECTION II.

APPLICATION OF METALLIC CONDUCTORS TO THE DEFENCE OF BUILDINGS AND SHIPPING FROM LIGHTNING.

Laws of Disruptive Discharges—Observed effects on Buildings and Shipping—Practical results of the preceding Inquiries—Nature and operation of Lightning Rods—Laws of Electrical Conduction—Mechanical effects of the Disruptive Discharge—What quantity of Metal is requisite in the construction of a Lightning Rod—How far does its protecting power extend.

SECTION II.

Laws and Operation of Disruptive Discharge.

WHATEVER may be the theoretical views entertained relative to the immediate source of lightning, and the manner in which disruptive electrical discharges occur in nature, it will be well to bear in mind, that all such discharges, have nevertheless one common character,—all produce similar effects,—and are all governed by the same laws. We propose, therefore, to consider these laws more particularly, with a view of arriving at certain practical deductions, immediately bearing on the question of the defence of buildings and shipping from lightning.

If we attentively examine the many recorded instances in which buildings and ships have been damaged by lightning, the course of the discharge may generally be traced; and this course is invariably determined through a given line or lines which, upon the whole, oppose the least resistance to the neutralization of the electrical forces. Both space and time are, as it were, economized in the restoration of the electrical equilibrium (pp. 4, 5); for however small we assume the duration of the discharge to be, or however limited the distance through which it strikes, both these quantities would become still less, were other lines of transit provided of still less resistance. This is the leading phenomenon of all disruptive discharges; hence lightning seizes upon such bodies as lie convenient and ready for its purpose, absolutely avoiding other bodies, however near, from which it can receive no assistance. And it may be further observed, as a most wonderful and interesting fact, that at the instant before the explosion takes place, the stream of electricity, in the act of moving to restore the equilibrium of distribution, feels its way as it were in advance, and absolutely marks out the course it is about to take, an inductive action being impressed upon such bodies as happen to lie in the line or lines of least resistance; this previous induction, by a sort of foresight, determines the course of the discharge. Its progress therefore is not, as many imagine, left to the chances of the instant, to be, as it were, attracted or drawn aside by metallic bodies at any given point; on the contrary, the whole course of a stroke of lightning is already fixed and settled, before the discharge takes place.

The evidence deducible from observation as well as from physical investigation, is most conclusive on this point. It is quite clear, from what has been already shown (p. 15), that any artificial elevation on the earth's surface is, in respect of a thunderstorm, a mere point in one of the terminating planes of a great electrical disturbance. The electrical forces cannot therefore be supposed to operate exclusively between such an elevation and a charged cloud. A building or ship, is struck by lightning only in consequence of its being a point in one of the electrified surfaces; in short, a heterogeneous mass, accidentally placed in a position to facilitate the neutralization of the electrical forces in a given direction, extending, perhaps, over many square miles of cloud and opposed sea or land (p. 55).

FIG. 10.

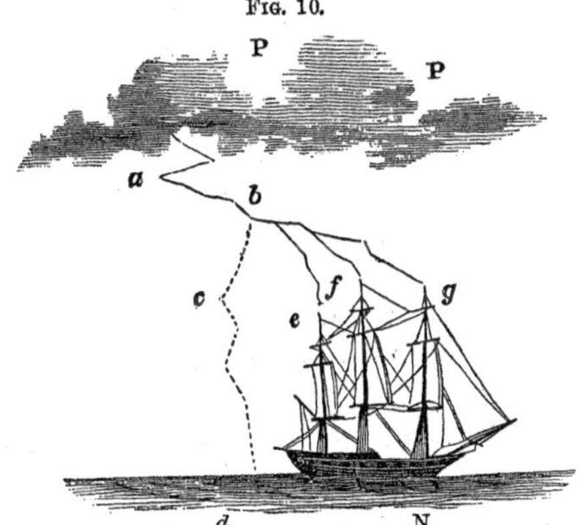

By way of illustration, let P N (fig. 10) represent the opposed terminating surfaces of the clouds and sea at the time of a thunderstorm, and N the position of a ship at the instant of discharge; let *a b* be the point, in which from any determining cause, the particles of the intervening air give way. Imagine further, that there were presented for the course of the discharge, such lines of transit, as *a b c d*, *a b e* N, *a b f* N, *a b g* N ; then the question, whether the ship N would be struck by lightning, would depend on the respective resistances, in the direction of these lines; it might so happen, that the resistance in the direction *a b c d*, although very near the vessel, might, from a variety of causes, be so much less than in any one of the other lines, that the discharge would not touch the ship at all. Conversely, the resistance might be *greater* in the direction *a b c d* than in any other, in which case the discharge would become determined through the ship, and one, two, or three, of the masts, would be struck by a division of the spark, in the way already stated (pp. 35, 36), according to the equality or difference of the resistance in these directions.

We must not, however, proceed too hastily without verifying principles by an appeal to experience: for however perfect theoretical views of such questions may be, it is still always desirable to adhere carefully to facts.

Her Majesty's cutter *Hawk*, was struck by lightning in Broadhaven Roads on the 21st of January, 1840, and seriously damaged. About the same time, the electrical discharge fell so near the *Neptune*, a small revenue cruiser at anchor in Ely Bay, as to cause the vessel to fairly reel by the concussion.* Her Majesty's ship *Southampton*, of fifty guns, experienced a heavy storm of lightning and thunder on the 30th of June, 1842, on the coast of South

* *Mayo Constitution.*

America, when a heavy electrical discharge fell so close to the ship, that it appeared to strike the main-chains.*

During the passage of Her Majesty's ship *Vanguard*, of eighty guns, from Portsmouth to the Mediterranean, in 1840, a dense explosion of lightning fell close upon the ship's quarter, without affecting the masts.†

The *Dart* steam-packet, whilst on her passage from London to Margate, in July, 1829, was exposed to a severe thunderstorm about five miles below the Nore. The electrical discharge struck the sea so near the vessel as to shake her considerably. One of the passengers stated that he saw a ball of fire fall into the water about twenty feet from the larboard side of the ship.‡

A great number of instances of this kind might be adduced in support of this important fact; it is however unnecessary to go at present into any further detail. We will therefore pass on to the track of the discharge, supposing it to be determined in the direction of the masts; and with a view of simplifying the question, we will select a common case in which it falls on one mast only, viz., on the main-mast, in the direction *a b f* N (fig. 10). In pursuing this course, the same general principle is apparent, *i. e.*, the electrical discharge is observed to fall on all those bodies which tend to assist its progress, and which happen to occupy certain relative positions,

* Master's log. † *Extract from private letter.*

‡ *Report of Commission on Shipwreck by Lightning*, p. 84.

and upon no others: attacking with destructive violence, imperfect conducting matter, and producing in various insulators, intermediate between good conductors, all the effects of a powerful expansive force. If we examine the course of any discharge of lightning, through a building or a ship, we shall find this effect invariable. The damage has always ensued where good conductors cease to be continued, and the destructive effects most apparent, are those commonly caused by an expansive force.

Observed Effects on Buildings and Ships.

The damage done by lightning to Her Majesty's ship *Rodney*, of ninety guns, may be adduced in illustration of this result in nature. This vessel, one of the finest of our line-of-battle ships in the Mediterranean, was struck by lightning on the 6th of December, 1838, off the south-east coast of Sicily, at 9 A. M. The electrical discharge fell on the vane-spindle, which was of wood, and on the truck at the mast-head. It then glanced over the royal pole to the head of the top-gallant mast, probably assisted by the moisture on its surface (p. 48); here it fell on a copper funnel, sixteen inches long and ten inches in diameter, placed on the mast for the support of the rigging. The resistance through the air, over the surface of the mast, seems to have been greater than through the wood; hence the top-gallant mast was shivered; it now seized upon the metals about the head of the topmast, and also on some men there on the cross-trees. From thence it struck over the surface of the topmast to the metallic bodies about the parrel of the topsail-yard, and so passed *per saltum* to the lower mast, leaving it in a tottering state. The expansive effect was so great, that thirteen of the iron hoops were burst open: about seven feet above the deck the concentrated shock divided; one portion passed over the hammock nettings into the sea; a second seized upon a metallic pump used for washing decks, and passed along the course of it through the ship's side, a third division passed below to the orlop deck, and through the metallic bodies in the hull, leaving the ship between decks full of a sulphurous odor and an apparent smoke. In this course, the discharge evidently sought assistance from all the conducting matter it could find, viz., wet ropes, copper funnel for rigging, iron work, &c., about the topmast cap, men on the cross-trees, metallic bodies about the parrel of the topsail-yard, &c.; and between all these it produced destructive effects. The interrupted circuit is quite evident in this case. It is traceable, first, to the copper funnel; secondly, from thence to the conducting bodies at the heel of the top-gallant mast; thirdly, from thence to the metallic masses about the yard; fourthly, between this and the head of the lower mast; fifthly, from this point over the iron hoops on the lower mast; lastly, to the hull and sea. The circumstance of the discharge striking over some portions of the mast without damage, is quite in accordance with all the known laws of electrical action already described (p. 48); thus a trace of water will allow a highly-charged jar to explode over a slip of glass without damage; and Dr. Franklin found he could not destroy a wet rat by artificial electricity, although he could a dry one, in consequence of the moisture conducting the charge over the surface of the body.

The following cases of damage by lightning, which have recently occurred in London are worthy of attentive consideration, inasmuch as the facts are still present to us, and the evidence they furnish of the course of electrical discharges is very complete. They have therefore been somewhat minutely described.

St. Martin's Church, struck by Lightning, 28*th July,* 1842.

Before tracing the course of the electrical discharge through the tower of this beautiful building, it will be requisite briefly to notice the position of the various rooms and substances through which it passed, together with such other circumstances as bear immediately on the great points under consideration.

A section of this tower is given in figs. 11 and 12. The spire, S C A, terminates in an iron rod, C A, formed into a spindle at its extreme point, for the support of the vane, A. This rod is from four inches and a half to five inches square, and about twenty-seven feet in length. It projects about twelve feet into the air, and passes fifteen feet into the spire through a gilded ball of copper, thirty-three inches in diameter, and one-sixteenth of an inch thick, and through two solid blocks of stone. It is supported within by a strong cross of iron, let into the masonry at *c* (fig. 11). The weight of the bar is about twelve cwt. and three-quarters, and its extreme point about two hundred feet from the ground. There are other iron crosses in the interior of the spire, besides that supporting the spindle of the vane, as at *t* and *v* (fig. 11): these serve as cramps to the masonry; they are not connected with each other. The vane at A is constructed of sheet copper, well gilded, and is about eight feet long and six feet wide.

The spire is a light hollow structure, forty-four feet high, standing on an open cupola, and surrounded by ornamental columns and arches. The floor of this cupola is covered with lead, and there is a massive framework of wood and iron, resting on it. This frame is constructed in two parts, for the support of a flagstaff F, one of which can be pushed out clear of the tower when required. Beneath the cupola is the dial-room *f*, containing the iron spindles of the clock faces, as at *e f n*. The figures marking the hours constitute portions of the stone-facing which surrounds the recesses of the circles forming the centre of the dials: these circles are formed of shutters of wood and iron, in eight divisions, and are painted black. The four cross rods at *e f* (fig. 12,) carry the hour and

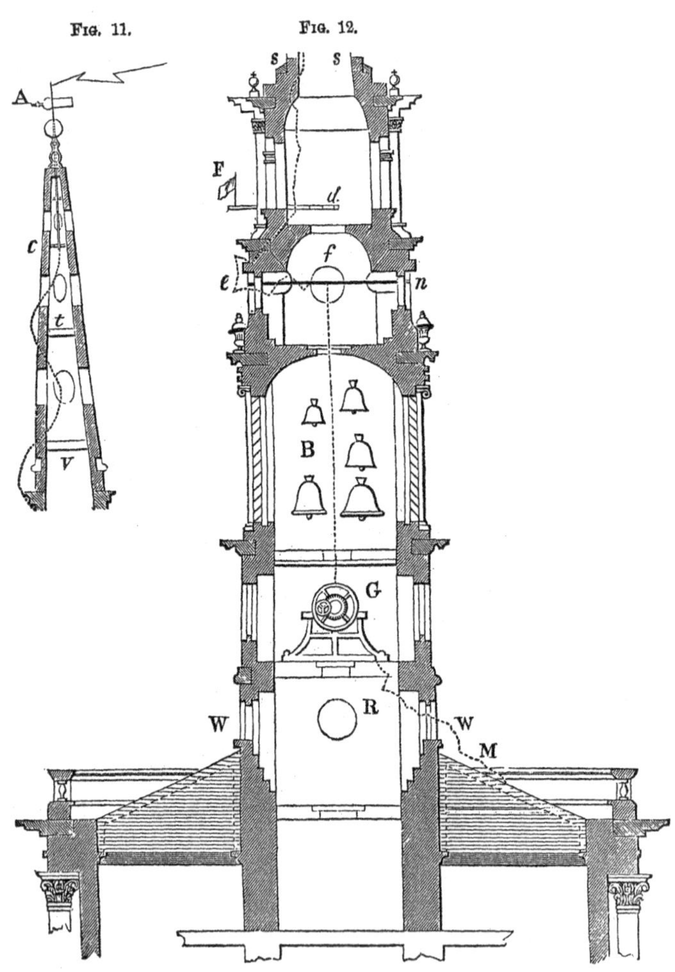

Fig. 11. Fig. 12.

minute hands of each dial, and are supported in the middle of the dial-room *f*, without touching the walls.

Under the dial-room is the belfry B, in which are the bells, suspended in frames in the usual way; they weigh from five to thirty-one cwt. Beneath the belfry is the clock-room G; the clock in this room is supported in a massive iron frame fixed to the floor; an iron rod *f* G, about three-fourths of an inch in diameter, and forty-six feet long, passes from the wheel-work up through the belfry B to the spindles at *f*, by which the requisite motion is conveyed to the hands on the dial-plates; this rod is constructed of several pieces, united by brass screws: it is cased in wood, and passes within ten inches of the lip of each bell.

Beneath the clock-room is the ringing-chamber R, having windows W W′ with iron frames; immediately without these is the lead, covering the roof of the church, as at M.

We have now before us almost every particular requisite to a clear comprehension of the track, and phenomena of the electrical explosion which fell on this fine structure.

The first point struck was the point of the vane-spindle at A; the discharge passed into the spire through the rod A C, without any damage to the blocks of stone immediately surrounding it, and without affecting the copper ball or the gilding of the vane. The only effect produced was the disturbance of a little cement about the ball, which seemed as if shaken by a violent concussion of the air. At the cross *c* the discharge left the vane-rod, and passed into the masonry of the spire, starting an angle stone, and from thence so damaged the spire in passing down it, as to leave the whole in a tottering state. Two blocks of stone were thrown completely out of their places, and fell through the roof into the church, the joints of the spire were all loosened, and its general surface contorted. Two other stones were quite dislocated; if these had also been thrown out, the whole of the upper portion of the spire must have fallen. From the base of the spire, the discharge fell with destructive violence upon the frame-work of the flagstaff at *d*, the wood-work of which was shivered, and then seizing the lead floor of the cupola, it forced a passage to a metal clamp within the masonry, where it tore up and fractured a large flat stone, and turned it completely over; in this way it passed to the nearest points outside the tower leading to the north and west dials: upon these the discharge divided, and fell upon the gilded letters XI. and XII., the gold of which, on the west dial more especially, was burnt up and blackened. From these points it exploded upon the minute-hands; here it also blackened the gold, and damaged the points of the hands. From this, it passed along the spindles of the north and west dials into the dial-room, without affecting the surrounding parts, and seizing the iron rod *f* G, connecting the spindles with the clock, it passed safely within its case of wood, and between the masses of metal in the bells down to the works of the clock: the only traces left in this course, were a little fusion of the brass screws, and of the iron at the union of the joints. The discharge, on reaching the works of the clock, melted a small copper wire by which the lever handle key was suspended on the iron frame: it now spread over the wheels and other parts, magnetized the steel pivots, blackened the silver face of the regulator, and burst open the door of the outer wooden casing,—it did not, however, stop the clock. The discharge, on leaving these conductors, forced a passage through the floor of the clock-room G by the assistance of some metal clamps, into the ringing chamber R, leaving the floor as if blown up by gunpowder. Coming out just over one of the iron window-frames W, it shattered all the glass in the window by the violent concussion, and left marks of fusion on small streaks of lead in the joints of the stones. By this course it reached the lead of the roof at M, and slightly fused it at the point on which the discharge first fell. After this it became dispersed upon the earth without further damage, by the large masses of metal and pipes connecting the roof with the ground.

It is impossible to conceive a case giving a better insight into the nature of disruptive discharges, through a fortuitous arrangement of good and imperfect conductors, than this now before us. In the first place, we may observe that all the damage has occurred in points where good conducting matter ceases to be continued,—as for example, between the termination of the vane-rod at *c* and the clock-faces at *c* and *f*, and again between the works of the clock at G and the lead of the roof at M, whilst the course of the discharge in the irregular line A *c s d e f* B G W M, is so marked and definite, and so independent of bodies not contributing to assist its progress, that we perceive it actually passing down the small iron rod *f* G within a few inches of the bells, without affecting in any way these large metallic masses, or disturbing the wooden case by which the rod was surrounded. The discharge in passing upon the dials, selected the north and west faces as affording the easiest line of transit, and as the minute hands only could contribute to the conduction, being at the time in a position to transmit it to the centre of the dial, these only were affected; the hour hands, although in continuation with the lower part of the dials, were evidently without the line of action: the course of the discharge, therefore, became diverted at right angles nearly from the line of the hands in order to pass upon the line of metals within the tower, thus completely coinciding with the phenomena of artificial discharge.*

* Every care has been taken to verify the facts of this case. Mr. Watkins, Optician, Charing Cross, London, well known as a careful observer of such phenomena, made a personal observation of the spire soon after the lightning fell on it, and very kindly furnished the result of his inquiries. Mr. R. Dyer, of the Norfolk Hotel, Surrey-street, also devoted much attention to the subject, and obtained from those immediately connected with the church every particular that could be desired. Mr. Newberry, the steeple-keeper, Mr. Hennings, the builder, and Mr. Langstaffe, who re-

Brixton Church, struck by Lightning, 24*th April*, 1842.

The course of this discharge is traced in fig. 13, which represents a section of the tower. There is a metallic cross V on the summit of the dome; this cross is of sheet copper, four and a half feet in height, and five inches square, and is supported by an iron bar, which passes within the cross through the masonry of the dome, and is secured by a nut at N. The masonry of the dome is very massive, and the joints of the stonework are strengthened by lead solderings. The dome is supported by stone columns about twelve feet high, as at M. Immediately under the cupola is the clock-room C, the roof of which is of wood covered with lead; C is the position of the clock: the works communicate with the dial-plates by means of iron rods, as D C half an inch in diameter. D is the position of one of the four clock-faces; the dial-plates are of sheet copper, about four feet in diameter, and the figures for the hours, &c., are covered with leaf gold. The works of the clock communicate with two bells at B by a small iron wire about thirty feet long, and one-tenth of an inch in diameter; this wire is not continuous, but made up of several pieces looped together; it is supported by means of small staples against an upright of wood. The bells at B are very close to each other: they are

gilt the vane, &c., gave freely all the information in their power. T. Morris, Esq. architect, also contributed much valuable information.

quite clear of the walls and the floor, and the larger one is always in connection with the clock by the wire *f i*,—in fact, the striking weight rests on it, being raised by the wire to strike the hour. Beneath

Fig. 13.

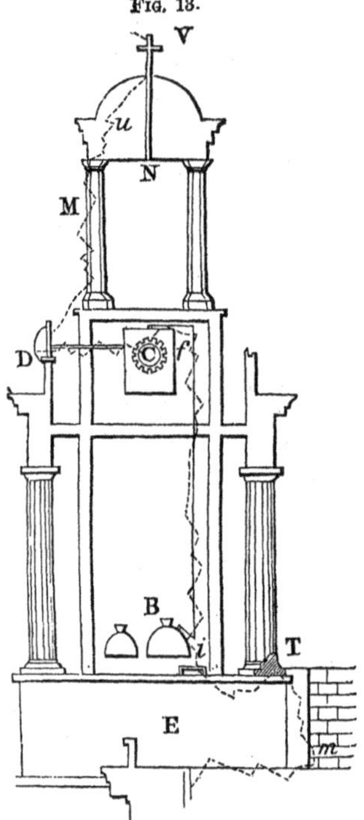

the belfry B is a room E communicating with it by a trap; there is an iron clamp, *i*, under the floor, about fifteen inches from the bell, and immediately outside, at about a foot distant, is the base of one of the ornamental columns T, which surround the middle portion of the tower. There are sixteen of these columns, and they are about eighteen feet long. At the base of column T is the lead-work *m* descending over the roof, and connected with the earth by metallic gutters and pipes. On reviewing the position of these different parts, we cannot but be struck with the analogy in their electrical relation to similar parts in St. Martin's spire, just described; we should accordingly expect to find precisely similar effects, and such is really the case, the course of the discharge being as follows.

The explosion fell first on the cross V, and followed it down to the masonry of the dome; there it diverged and rent the dome completely open, then finding its way along the inner side of one of the columns M, it slightly damaged the stone-work in the vicinity. It now reached the metals on the dials, and passed to the works of the clock at C by the iron rods D C, and from thence along the wire and wooden upright *f i* to the bell B; this wire was knocked to pieces, and portions of it dissipated. From the termination of the wire it burst upon the floor and clamp at *i*, as the shortest and easiest course to the lead *m* on the roof of the church. Exploding upon this point, it produced, by a common law of electrical action, so much expansion as to shatter the base of the column T; the wood of the floor also at the clamp *i* was torn up, as in St. Martin's spire, but with less damage; after this the discharge found its way to the earth, with but little further difficulty. The interrupted circuit traceable here, is represented by the irregular line V *u* M D C *f i* T, &c., and the disruptive discharge is precisely of the same character and description as that just described (p. 82).*

In every instance of damage to buildings or shipping by lightning, the course of the electrical discharge is determined in a similar way, through points presenting the least resistance to its progress, and the mischief invariably occurs between detached masses of metal. The beautiful steeple of St. Bride's Church in London, struck by lightning in June, 1764, furnishes a most remarkable instance of this. The spire of this steeple, where it rises above the belfry, is composed of four stories of different orders of architecture, beside the obelisk immediately over them. The stone piers of these stories are connected together and strengthened by horizontal iron bars; near the height of the capital of the pilasters, each story has a set of four bars, placed crosswise, and tied together by chain bars within the stone work. The obelisk

* The facts connected with this case have been minutely detailed by Mr. C. V. Walker, and there is not the slightest doubt of their accuracy. It is, however, proper to observe, that in the account given by Mr. Walker, he supposes a great portion of the charge to have passed *outside* the building by an iron pipe, because the damage done at the point *i* was not, he thinks, adequate to the force of the shock as experienced at the base of the column T. This supposition, however, is not warranted by any trace of the discharge in the direction Mr. Walker has pointed out, and must, therefore, be so far regarded as hypothetical. His account of this case, however, is singularly clear and instructive.

terminates in seven courses of stone, the five upper ones being connected together at the top and bottom by iron collars soldered with lead. An iron bar, about twenty feet in length and two inches square, passes through these for about ten feet in a groove cut through the middle of the solid stones and filled in with lead. This bar rests in the two solid stones of the lower courses, in which it is sunk five inches deep, and is further secured by melted lead. The upper part of the bar is cylindrical, and covered for about ten feet by a ball and cross, and by a vane, all of gilded copper. To lessen the quantity of stone in this beautiful structure, cramps of iron are employed in several places, on which ornamental stones are placed. Other iron bars are also employed to support the top of the windows, so that a more complete series of discontinuous metallic bodies intermixed with imperfect conducting matter, cannot well be conceived.

When the lightning struck this steeple, it made successive leaps between these metallic bodies, rending and tearing up the masonry at the points where it entered and again left them; so that it was requisite to rebuild eighty-five feet of the spire. One of the iron bars in the composite story was found broken in two, and another bent to an angle of nearly forty-five degrees. No damage whatever was done to the iron spindle, the vane or cross, or to the solid stones through which the iron bar passed. The gilding on the top of the cross, at the place where the discharge first struck, was the only part affected; this was either dissipated or discolored: a little solder also was melted at this spot, which appeared as if acted on by fire. The lightning, it is clear, entered here upon the whole metallic mass, and was quietly conducted to the termination of the iron spindle in the two lower courses of stone: its destructive operation now commenced, and the destruction was repeated at each successive leap between the disconnected metallic substances employed in the construction of the spire. The last trace of it was at the west window of the belfry, from whence it appears to have found an adequate conduction to the earth.*

Before concluding these notices, it may not be unimportant to detail, briefly, two cases of damage by lightning which exhibit in a remarkable way its destructive effects at sea and on shore, and show still further, the absolute necessity of guarding against them.

The frontispiece represents the condition of the *Thisbe*, an English frigate, struck by lightning in January 1786, near the Scilly Isles, during her passage from Lisbon to England. The weather at the time was tempestuous and squally, with showers of hail, so that the ship was hove-to under storm stay-sails.† The electrical discharge, after disabling several of the crew, struck on the mainmast, and set the sails and rigging on fire: it also struck the foremast and shivered it.‡ To get clear of the burning mass,

* *Phil. Trans.* for 1764, pp. 201 and 227.

† Ship's log. ‡ Idem.

the master cut one of the lanyards of the main shrouds to windward, when the force of the gale carried the whole over the side, together with the mizen-topmast; the fore-topmast soon followed, so that the ship was left almost a total wreck. The electrical discharge knocked down several of the crew near the guns, and swept the decks. *

PRACTICAL RESULT OF THE PRECEDING INQUIRIES.

Nature of Lightning Rods.

The damage sustained by buildings and ships in thunderstorms being invariably found to occur in the spaces where good conductors of electricity cease to be continued, it became an important question in practical science, how far it would be desirable to provide at once a continuous line of conduction, through which the electrical discharge might be transmitted without any intermediate explosion, and consequently without damage to the general mass. An idea first suggested by the American philosopher,

* A similar result ensued in the *Lowestoffe*, a sister ship, in the Mediterranean, in 1796. This frigate was also dismasted, and left a mere wreck.

Franklin, and since carried effectually into practice under the form of a lightning rod.

The application of such a rod to a building or ship, is evidently equivalent to the uniting into a continuous conducting train, all the detached metallic masses between which damage ensues, and in the case of particular buildings, into the construction of which such masses do not enter, it supplies the degree of conducting power requisite for their safety. A conducting rod, therefore, in whatever way it may be applied, is to be considered merely as a means of perfecting the conducting power of the whole mass, so as to admit of intense discharges of lightning being securely transmitted, which otherwise would not pass without intermediate explosion and damage; for it must never be forgotten, as an important feature in the consideration of this question, that the materials of which buildings and ships are composed, are for the most part such as come under the denomination of conductors (p. 8); the whole fabric is, therefore, to a greater or less extent, an electrical conductor. Now the chance of its escaping damage from a discharge of lightning, increases with its power of transmitting the electrical action by which it is assailed. If we could suppose a ship or building to have a perfect conducting power in all its parts, or if we imagine it to be metallic throughout, then damage from lightning would be unknown. Thus discharges of lightning struck repeatedly on the iron steamboat which accompanied Lander in his last attempt to explore the interior of Africa, without producing the slightest effect on it; whilst vessels built of wood and metal were damaged. A man in armor would certainly be safe in a thunderstorm, from the great conducting power of the metal as compared with the human body. The great object, therefore, to be attained in the application of lightning conductors to the defence of buildings and shipping from lightning, is to bring the general mass as nearly into this state as possible.

It has already been observed (p. 9), that Mr. Cavendish determined the conducting power of iron to be, in relation to that of water, as four hundred millions to one. Taking therefore the conducting power of water as unity, and assuming it as the value of the mean conducting power of the general mass of a building, which is upon the whole not far from the truth, then, by giving a building a lightning conductor of great capacity, and connecting it with the detached masses of metal as far as is possible, we multiply its chance of escaping damage, in the intermediate points in which the conductor is applied, four hundred millions of times; and considering that by the laws of electrical action, the electrical discharge finds its way through any line or lines, which upon the whole offer the least resistance to its passage, nothing can be clearer than the deduction, that any incapacity of the building as a whole, to transmit the charge through its parts without explosion, would be supplied by the presence of the conductor; and hence this multiplied chance of escape applies equally to the whole building. It is therefore demonstrable by physical facts, that perfect security is to be derived from an efficient conductor properly applied.

The first lightning conductor seen in England, was erected by Dr. Watson at Payneshill, in 1762. In 1769 the Jacob tower at Hamburg was defended by a lightning rod, and after the cathedral church at Sienna had been repeatedly damaged by lightning, a similar means of protection was employed there also. The inhabitants at first regarded the rod with terror and apprehension, and called it a Heretic Rod; but on the 10th of April, 1777, a thunderstorm occurred, and there fell on the tower a heavy stroke of lightning, which was carried off by the rod, without doing the slightest damage even to the gilded ornaments near which it passed.* The inhabitants now began to look on the heretic rod with more confidence; and it is an important fact, that this church does not seem to have suffered from lightning since.

Laws of Electrical Conduction.

The heating effect of the same, or different quantities of electricity, on metallic wires of the same or different diameters, is as the square of the passing quantity of electricity directly, and as the square of the diameter of the wire inversely. Thus the heat developed by a passing shock is four times as great when the quantity of electricity is doubled, and only one-fourth as great when the diameter of the wire is doubled. A metallic rod, therefore, of twice the di-

* MARBUCH, *Enkyklopædie*, vol. i., p. 314.

ameter, conducts twice the quantity of electricity with the same development of heat. Taking the heat evolved as proportionate to the resistance, we may conclude, that the conducting power of a metallic body varies with the area exposed in cutting it transversely to its length; that is to say, with the area of its section, since this is proportionate to its solid contents.

In estimating the resistance of a metallic body to the transmission of a shock of electricity, we have also to take into consideration the distance traversed. Now the resistance to electrical transmission through a metallic wire, has been found to increase with the length of the wire; that is to say, the resistance to the transmission of the charge was twice as great when the length of the conductor was doubled; a law observable from one hundred up to one thousand feet in length. A lightning conductor, therefore, should have its dimensions increased, when required to be of considerable extent.

The explanation of the above general laws seems to be this: supposing a given quantity of electricity to fall on a single metallic particle, and to experience a given resistance to its progress, then this resistance would be diminished by placing a second particle by the side of it, for the charge would be divided between the two. If two other particles were added, we may conceive it to be still further reduced in proportion to the number of particles sharing in the conduction. Now, in the case of the section of a metallic wire, the diameter of which is double that of another, there are four times the number of particles,—hence the resistance with the same quantity of charge is reduced to one-fourth. In a similar way it may be shown, that by increasing the length of the conductor, we continually increase the number of particles to be passed through,—hence the resistance through twice the length will be twice as great, through three times the length three times as great, and so on. In the case of the quantity of electricity being increased, we have the resistance dependent not only on the increased charge, but also on its increased force. Thus a particle of metal conducting a double quantity of electricity is subject to a double force, since it is quite reasonable to conclude that the forces (p. 17) with which the opposite electrical powers tend to unite, would increase with the amount of disturbance.

Mechanical Effects of the Electrical Discharge.

But it is not only the heating effect of the discharge we have to consider; it is necessary to take also into the account its more mechanical effects,—indeed, it is the expansive action which produces the great mass of damage by lightning so commonly observed. If a powerful shock of electricity be transmitted by a fine wire, the wire will very often appear crippled throughout its length, and will exhibit a series of zigzag creases. And if a similar shock be passed between two metallic balls in a confined portion of air, the air will be caused to expand with great violence, so as to frequently burst open the containing vessel. Light bodies such as wafers will become dispersed in all directions, when exposed to the expansive effect produced by the electric shock in passing through a short interval of air.

At the time the steeple of St. Bride's church, London, was struck by lightning, in June, 1764, it is stated by Mr. Delaval, F.R.S., who communicated a most interesting detail of the circumstances to the Royal Society, that "the lightning acted as an elastic fluid," and that "the effects are exactly similar to those which would have been produced by gunpowder, pent up in the same places and exploded. A stone weighing about seventy pounds was thrown to a distance of fifty yards; an iron bar half an inch in thickness, and about two feet in length, joining some of the masonry of the tower, was not only broken in two, but one part of it, according to Dr. Watson,* was actually bent to an angle of 45°."

The mechanical effects of lightning, seen in piercing solid bodies with holes, in splitting them in pieces, and in projecting their fragments (sometimes of enormous weight) to great distances, are so well known, and so generally admitted, that it will be needless to multiply instances in proof of it; but a circumstantial statement of some remarkable cases of this kind may throw light upon the manner in which the electric fluid acts.

* *Phil. Trans.* for 1764.

In the autumn of 1778, lightning struck the house of Casselli, an engineer, at Alexandria. It did no damage, but pierced the panes of glass in the windows with several small holes about the sixth of an inch in diameter. Small cracks in the glass diverged from these holes as centres.

In August, 1777, lightning struck the steeple of the parish church of St. Sepulchre at Cremona, broke the iron cross which surmounted the tower, and projected to a distance the weathercock, which revolved under the cross, and which was made of copper, tinned, and coated with oil-paint.

This weathercock was found to have been pierced with *eighteen holes*, nine of which were very prominent on one side, and the other nine on the other. As there was no appearance of more than one stroke of lightning, all these holes must be supposed to have been pierced at once. The position of the holes are such as would have been produced by blows imparted simultaneously in opposite directions on parts of the metal nearly contiguous, and the inclination of the beards or projecting edges of the holes on one side correspond exactly with those on the other, the directions of all the eighteen beards being parallel.

On the 3d of July, 1821, lightning struck a house at Geneva, and pierced the tin which covered a part of the roof with several holes, leaving evident marks of fusion. One piece of tin in particular, which covered the angle made by a chimney with the surface of the roof near it, was pierced with three nearly circular holes, about an inch and three quarters in diameter, and about five inches apart, measured from centre to centre. The metal at the edges of these holes was bent, as it would have been by a force bursting through it in one direction or the other. The edges of the two holes were bent on contrary sides.

On the night between the 14th and 15th of April, 1718, the church of Gouesnon, near Brest, was struck by lightning with such force that it shook as if by an earthquake. The stones of the walls were projected in all directions to a distance of from fifty to sixty yards.

The lightning which formally struck the Chateau of Clermont, in Beauvoisis, made a hole twenty-six inches wide and the same depth in the wall; the date of the building of which was so far back as the time of Cæsar, and which was so hard that a pickaxe could with difficulty make any impression upon it.

On the night between the 21st and 22d of June, 1723, lightning struck a tree in the forest of Nemours. The trunk was split into two fragments, one seventeen, and the other twenty-two feet long. These fragments, so heavy that one of them would require the combined strength of four men, and the other that of eight men, to lift it, were, nevertheless, projected by the lightning to the distance of about seventeen yards.

In January, 1762, lightning struck the church of Breag, in Cornwall, the southwest pinnacle of the tower of which it destroyed. A stone, weighing one hundred and seventy pounds, was projected from the roof of the church to a distance of sixty yards in the direction of the south. Another fragment of stone was projected to the north to a distance of 400 yards. A third was projected to the southwest.

About the middle of the last century, a rock of micaceous schist, measuring 105 feet long, 10 feet wide, and about 4 feet thick, was struck by lightning at Funzie, in Scotland, and was broken into three principal fragments, not counting smaller pieces. One of these fragments twenty-six feet long, ten feet wide, and four feet thick, had been merely inverted in its position. Another, 28 feet long, 7 feet wide, and 5 feet thick, was projected over the hill to a distance of fifty yards. The remaining piece, forty feet long, was projected in the same direction, with still greater force, and fell into the sea.

On the 6th of August, 1809, at *Swinton*, about five miles from *Manchester*, lightning struck the house of Mr. Chadwick, at 2 P. M. A sulphurous vapor immediately filled the house. The external wall of a building erected against the house as a coal-shed, was torn from its foundations, and raised in a mass. It was transported, maintaining its vertical position, to some distance from its original place; one of its ends was transported nine and the other four feet. This wall thus raised and transported, was composed of seven thousand bricks, which, independent of the mortar by which they were cemented together, would have weighed about twenty-six tons. This wall was eleven feet high and three feet thick, and its foundation was about a foot below the level of the ground. Above this coal-shed was a cistern, which, at the time of the phenomenon, contained a quantity of water, and the shed contained about a ton of coals.*

The first Presbyterian church in the City of Syracuse, New-York, was struck by lightning. The church had lightning rods attached, but these were improperly fastened to the walls by sharp-pointed staples in full connection with the main rod. The lightning struck the spire, ran down part way, when the charge divided, following a staple fastening into the building, as far as the pointed staple extended. This staple terminating in the dry, hard masonry, which must have been nearly a non-conductor, the charge blasted out a portion of the steeple,—throwing the broken fragments several hundred feet, much after the manner of a too shallow blast in a rock. And thus the beautiful structure was saved the dire destruction which must have happened had the church been built of wood, a partial conductor when wet, and fastened with iron bolts, &c. These facts were related to the writer a few months since by several intelligent and respectable citizens of that city, who were eye-witnesses to the accident, each of whom saved pieces that were thus blasted out of the steeple. The mechanical force here manifested was precisely like that of gunpowder.

In the shock of lightning which fell on His Majesty's ship *Elephant*, of seventy-four guns, at

* Dr. Lardner's Lect. on Science and Art, vol. ii. p. 69.

Portsmouth, in November, 1790, all the iron hoops and wooldings on the mainmast were burst open and broken in pieces, and some of the parts scattered to great distances. Some of these hoops were half an inch thick, and five inches wide; the mast, although of immense size, being about three feet in diameter, and upwards of 110 feet in length, was entirely shook and shivered throughout.* Now, in these cases we do not find any melting of the iron work: we observe only the effects of a terrific mechanical power.

Another remarkably interesting instance of this effect was observed in the case of His Majesty's ship *Desirée*, already alluded to (p. 55), struck by lightning in Port Antonio, in Jamaica, in the autumn of 1803. Admiral Ross, who then commanded the ship, states, that one part of the main-topmast was found on the following morning sticking in the mud on one side of the harbor, and another part in a timber-yard on the opposite side.

In the application of lightning conductors to buildings, therefore, we have to consider the effect likely to be produced on them by the mechanical action of the shock, by which they may be disjointed, twisted, or rent asunder in various ways. Thus, the small conductor of linked brass rod, at Charles Church, Plymouth, struck by lightning in December, 1824, was literally torn in pieces and disjointed, and many of the links twisted into the shape of the

* *Naval Chronicle.*

letter S. A part of the small wire rope applied as a conductor to the Hotel des Invalides at Paris was broken into small pieces an inch or more in length, and scattered in all directions by the lightning which fell on that building in June, 1839. This conductor consisted of about twenty iron wires twisted together as a rope; the lead surrounding the lantern was torn up and scattered, but without any signs of fusion.*

The intensity of electrical accumulation having been found to decrease in an inverse ratio of the square of the opposed surfaces, some electricians were led to imagine that extent of surface was the great desideratum in the application of a lightning conductor. This decrease of intensity, however, does not affect the conditions of conduction as regards the heating effect of the discharge, for, whether the quantity of electricity be accumulated on a large extent of surface, or on a small one, the

* *Comptès Rendus*, June 17, 1839.

A question of no small public interest arises here relative to the insurance of buildings against lightning, which has been assumed to be a *species of fire*, and that hence all buildings damaged by lightning are damaged as if by fire: but this is certainly not the case. A building may be struck by lightning, and may certainly be set on fire by it; but in the great variety of cases which occur, the damage is purely of a mechanical kind: thus, in the case of the spire of St. Martins, already described, no damage could be said to have arisen from fire, and consequently no responsibility could attach to those who assured it against fire only; the damage was purely mechanical, and must be classified with the kind of damage occurring from a heavy gale of wind, or any other mechanical force.

heating effect, when the discharge does occur, is always the same. Whatever may be the distance at which the neutralization of the forces begins, they always unite with precisely the same degree of power, the quantity of electricity being the same.

This question, so frequently discussed, has not been fully appreciated in all its details, for although quantity of metal is an essential condition of a lightning rod, yet it is likewise desirable to place the metallic particles under as great an extent of surface as may be consistent with strength and durability, in order to keep down the intensity of the shock, and diminish the mechanical action. We may, in fact, for the moment, consider a conductor, while in the act of carrying off a charge of lightning, as an electrified body. Its electrical intensity, therefore, is very much less with a large surface than with a small one: hence, by extent of surface, we diminish the activity of the passing charge, and tranquillize its mechanical effect on the conductor. Thus we find, in a variety of cases of damage by lightning, that the passing charge, in striking on large expanded sheets of metal, has become comparatively tranquil, and has been traced no further, whilst in striking on larger masses of metal, exposing but a small surface, it has assumed an intensely active state. The flash of lightning which struck His Majesty's ship *Badger*, lying in the Medway, in August, 1822, vanished, after striking upon the copper lining of the galley, although just before, it had penetrated the mast, rent the copper, and melted the lead over the heads of two large bolts in the deck beams.

Although the general tendency of a discharge of lightning is always through the conductor, as being the line of least resistance (p. 69), yet there may arise cases in which the electrical forces may be so circumstanced as to affect other lines of action near it, and in which damage may ensue. Thus, in the French frigate *Calypso*, fitted with a wire conductor of small surface, two men in the main chains, who were standing in a slightly interrupted conducting communication between the wire and the sea, were struck senseless. A similar case is related by M. Arago, as having occurred in the French frigate *Junon*. In fact, wherever from any cause the resistance in the direction of the conductor is considerable, the chances of damage in some other direction become multiplied. Thus, a case occurred at Bayonne, in which the length of the conductor was unnecessarily increased,—that is to say, instead of terminating at once in the ground, it was led off at the foot of the building on semi-insulating stakes of wood for some distance; the charge here divided upon other lines near the conductor, and caused damage.*

Provided the quantity of metal be present, the form under which we place it is evidently of no consequence to its conducting power,† since it would be

* *Annuaire* pour 1838, p. 597.

† The reader will observe that the writer is speaking of the capacity of metal to conduct a *given amount* of electricity, without regard to power to disperse or weaken the charge by edges and points.

absurd to suppose that a mass of metal, under any form, did not conduct electricity in all its particles,—indeed, we know that it does so, and that it is impossible to fuse by electricity *a portion only* of a homogeneous metallic plate of uniform thickness. Again, if the heating effect of a given quantity of electricity on a metallic wire be measured, and then the wire be rolled out into a flat surface, or otherwise drawn out and placed under the form of two or more smaller ones, still the same heat will be evolved when conducting the same charge; * there is consequently no disadvantage in giving a lightning rod as much superficial capacity as possible as regards conducting power, whilst, on the contrary, the diminished intensity attendant on it is very advantageous: this effect of superficial conductors appears to depend on the removal of the electrical particles further out of the sphere of each other's influence. In a dense solid rod they may be supposed to be in a state of compression, in each other's way, as it were,—whereas, by expanding the same quantity of metal into a larger surface, we immediately free them from this condition, and allow them greater space.†

In order, therefore, to resist the heating effect, we require quantity of metal; to restrain the electrical intensity, and to diminish the mechanical force, we require extent of surface. The distinction is nice, but it is a very important one.

* *Trans. Royal Society* for 1827.

† See *Phil. Trans.* for 1834 and 1836, pp. 232 and 450, for some further inquiries on this point by the author.

Two questions here present themselves which demand attentive consideration, viz., what quantity of metal is requisite to perfect security, and to what extent will a lightning rod afford protection,—in other words, what is the sphere of its influence? These problems, although apparently difficult, admit of a satisfactory solution—a solution, it is true, depending on the results of experience, but still perfectly conclusive; for it is here to be remembered, that we seek protection not against discharges of lightning which have no existence out of the imagination, but against such as have fallen within the experience of mankind—not against convulsions of nature, in which it would probably be of little consequence whether we had lightning rods or not, but against probable and tangible results of the operation of a given natural agency, with the laws of which we are ill acquainted. Now, we have the recorded experience of more than a century to guide us in this inquiry; and first, with respect to the actual quantity of electricity which may be contained in a flash of lightning, and the quantity of metal requisite to resist its effects.

What quantity of Metal is requisite for a Lightning Rod?

Perhaps one of the most terrific discharges of lightning ever experienced, was that in the case of the New-York packet, struck by lightning in the

Gulf Stream, in April 1827, already noticed (p. 54). In this case the discharge fell on a pointed iron rod four feet long, and half an inch in diameter; some few inches only of the rod near its point were melted; the linked iron chain which descended from this rod to the water, about a quarter of an inch in diameter, was knocked in pieces by the expansive force of the shock, and some of the links fused. The flash of lightning not only melted some of the links, but "caused them to burn like a taper." "The melted iron fell in glowing drops upon the deck, which was instantly set on fire wherever the burning matter fell." "Such was the violence of the shock, that the ship recoiled, or, in sea phrase, lurched so strongly, as to throw down the people on the deck."* The results of a great natural experiment are here presented to us, and we see that an iron rod of half an inch in diameter, effectually resisted a flash which fused and destroyed a chain of about one half of its dimensions.

The flash of lightning which struck Her Majesty's ship *Rodney*, in December 1838, was so powerful that it quite dispersed the topgallant-mast in small chips, covering the sea with splinters, set fire to the main-topsail, tore a piece ten feet long out of the topmast, burst thirteen hoops on the mainmast, each five inches wide and half an inch thick, and traversed the mast with destructive effect for fifty-three feet. Now this charge passed without fusion on the cop-

* *Report of Commission on Shipwreck by Lightning.*

per funnel, sixteen inches long, ten inches in diameter, and less than a quarter of an inch thick, belonging to the topgallant rigging.

In September 1833, two successive discharges of lightning fell on His Majesty's ship *Hyacinth*, in the Indian Ocean, and descended by the fore and main-masts to the sea. The topgallant and topmasts were literally shaken into a bundle of laths, so that they could scarcely be supported; the topmasts thus shivered were from eleven to twelve inches in diameter and about forty feet in length. This destructive shock was safely conducted away from the termination of the topmasts by a chain sheet fifty feet long, made of iron rod half an inch in diameter, and finally through the ship by a copper pipe, three inches in diameter, one-eleventh of an inch thick, and ten feet long; * before reaching these bodies, which were direct conductors to the sea, the discharge ravaged and destroyed the masts through a distance of nearly eighty feet; the chain did not show any marks of fusion.

In the summer of the year 1760, a heavy discharge fell on a conductor fixed on a house in Philadelphia. This conductor consisted of an iron rod, half an inch in diameter; it extended nine feet above the chimneys, and terminated in an iron stake in the ground. The part above the chimneys was tipped with brass rod, about a quarter of an inch in diameter, and ten inches long. Mr. West, the owner of

* *Report of Commission on Lightning Rods*, p. 44.

the house, judging from the crash that the conductor had been struck, had it examined. About three inches of the brass rod were observed to have been fused, and some of the fused metal had sunk down about the remaining part of the rod, forming a rough, irregular cap about it. The house was not damaged, nor were any further effects produced on the conductor.*

On the 26th of January, 1838, a flash of lightning fell on Her Majesty's ship *Dublin*, of fifty guns, at Rio de Janeiro. It was carried off by a conductor of long copper links, each link being about a quarter of an inch in diameter, and ten inches long. The conductor was "regularly melted" in several parts; these fell on the deck; other parts, which remained attached to the line supporting the chain along the rigging of the ship, appeared as if they had been exposed to a very fierce heat. This line was not hurt, nor was any damage done to the rigging.†

A house was struck by lightning at Tenterden, on the 17th of June, 1774. The discharge was conducted by an iron bar three-quarters of an inch square, but produced no effect on it.‡

In June, 1772, a discharge of lightning fell on the Vicarage-house at Steeple Ashton, in Wiltshire. The iron bell-wires in both the parlors and in the

* *Phil. Trans.*, vol. liii. part 1.

† *Report on Shipwreck by Lightning*, p. 94.

‡ *Phil. Trans.* for 1775.

hall were entirely dispersed, *except in their twisted or double portions.**

In June, 1828, a heavy flash of lightning fell on the spire of Kingsbridge church, in Devonshire, and was received on an iron spindle, seven feet long, and one inch in diameter, without producing the least effect on it, or damaging the stones around it: but on leaving the spindle, however, it shattered the tower, and did considerable damage.

In the case of Charles church at Plymouth (p. 100), although the wire was knocked in pieces at the points of junction, and considerably bent, it was not materially damaged by fusion.

"In reviewing, in this way, a great variety of cases in which buildings and ships have been exposed to appalling storms of lightning in various parts of the world, and throughout a century of years, we are enabled to appreciate the power of metallic bodies to carry off lightning with safety. Now we do not find in any of these cases that a conducting rod, or other mass of metal, equal in substance or conducting power to a rod of copper half an inch in diameter and six inches long, has ever been fairly melted. On the contrary, heavy discharges have traversed rods of less dimensions with safety."

Besides, the conducting power of lightning rods has been much increased of late by improvements in their construction. 1st. In multiplying the number

* *Phil. Trans.* for 1773.

of their points. 2d. In perfecting their continuity. 3d. In the substitution of square rods for round ones. The reasons of these facts will appear hereafter. We will here stop only to add, what Mr. Harris, F. R. S., in his work on thunderstorms, affirms, viz., "when an acutely terminated lightning rod receives a charge of lightning, a very considerable portion of the charge, if not the whole, runs off in an attenuated stream."

How far does the Protecting Power of a Lightning Rod extend?

It is not easy to assign the limit of the protecting power of a conductor. The French philosophers consider it will afford protection over a circle equal to twice its radius;* this, although possible in certain cases, is by no means a general truth. All the experience we have of the operation of conductors on discharges of lightning, tends to the conclusion, that they have no influence whatever in determining the course of such discharges, further than arises out of the circumstance of their furnishing an easy line of conduction. That they do not always afford protection over any considerable distance, is clear from the following cases:—

Her Majesty's ship *Endymion*, commanded by Captain the Honorable F. Grey, was struck by lightning at Calcutta, in March, 1842. This frigate had

* *Annales de Chimie et de Physique*, vol. 26.

a chain conductor on the mainmast, applied in the usual way, not very dissimilar to that recommended in the report of M. Gay Lussac to the Royal Academy of Sciences at Paris. The electrical explosion, instead of falling on the conductor, struck the foremast, shivered the top-gallant and topmast, and damaged the lower mast. Now, in this case, the mast struck was not above fifty feet distant from the mainmast, which was furnished with a conductor, and had a radius of one hundred and fifty feet.*

Her Majesty's ship *Ætna* was struck by several heavy electrical discharges at Corfu, in January, 1830. These, for the most part, passed down a chain conductor attached to the mainmast. One of the discharges, however, struck the ship near the bow, and exploded about twelve feet above the forecastle, close to the foremast, knocking down all the people on deck, and doing other damage.†

The Board-house, at Purfleet, was struck by lightning on the 12th of May, 1777,‡ at a point upwards of forty feet from the conductor with which the house was furnished. The damage, it is true, was small; a few stones fastened by iron cramps not connected with the conductor were thrown down. The Board-house was a lofty building, with a pointed roof, well leaded, and connected by lead gutters and pipes with the earth, and with wells forty feet deep, for the purpose of conveying water forced up to a

* Ship's log, and private letter.

† Ship's log. ‡ *Phil. Trans.*

cistern in the roof. It was therefore only thought necessary to add an iron spike, about ten feet long, to the middle of the highest part of the roof. About one hundred and fifty yards from this building were five powder magazines, each one hundred and sixty feet long and fifty-two feet wide, having spiked conductors at each end, projecting ten feet above the roofs, and connected with wells of water. It is quite apparent here, that so far as relates to the *influence* of a conductor over a given area, the experiment is conclusive, and the result shows that we cannot always calculate on the radius of protection; thus confirming the deductions already arrived at* (p. 72).

The Poor-house at Heckingham was struck by lightning on the 17th of June, 1781, which damaged one of the extreme corners of the building, situate seventy feet from the pointed conductors with which the house was furnished. Little or no damage, however, was sustained. The house consisted of a central range of buildings and two flanks; in general form, approaching that of the letter H. There were eight chimneys; each had a pointed conductor. The flash appears to have divided in this case before reaching the ground (p. 35). One portion struck on one of the conductors, and was carried off; a second struck the extreme point of the building, and set it on fire; a third fell on the earth immediately in front of it.†

The house at Tenterden, already referred to (p.

* *Phil. Trans.* for 1773. † *Phil. Trans.*, vol. lxxii., p. 377.

108), had two stacks of chimneys at each end. To one of these stacks was fixed a conductor of iron rod, projecting five feet above the chimney. Now, the discharge fell on one of the chimneys fifty feet distant, at the opposite end of the building; being the chimney diagonally opposite to that on which the conductor was placed, and on passing to the earth, it did considerable damage. The whole of this shock was finally concentrated on an iron bar three-quarters of an inch square, and produced no effect on it, as already noticed (p. 108). The house was about thirty feet wide.*

These cases evidently throw doubt on any theoretical calculation as to the limit of distance, within which a pointed lightning conductor will afford protection, and confirm in a remarkable way the views we have taken of electrical discharges from the atmosphere (p. 69)

* *Phil. Trans.*, 1775.

SECTION III.

RESULTS OF THE APPLICATION OF LIGHTNING RODS TO BUILDINGS AND SHIPS,

FROM THE PERIOD OF THEIR FIRST BEING EMPLOYED IN THE YEAR 1760.

Introductory Remarks.—Whether Metallic Conductors have effectually defended Buildings, &c. against Lightning?—Whether Lightning Rods attract Lightning?—Whether pointed Conductors actually prevent explosions of Lightning?—The Phenomena observed, when concentrated discharge strikes upon a Conducting Rod.—Harmless character of the luminous appearances observed on Lightning Rods.—Division of the Charge.—Instances in which Buildings having pointed Lightning Rods are said to have been damaged by Lightning.—Precautions when exposed to the action of Thunderstorms.—Construction of Lightning Rods applied to Buildings.—Practical Deductions.—Concluding Observations.

SECTION III.

Introductory Remarks.

In the preceding sections we have considered the physical conditions of a thunderstorm, and the laws and mode of operation of electrical discharges. From these inquiries we have deduced certain practical results relative to the employment of metallic substances under the form of lightning rods, as a means of protection against the calamitous effects of lightning.

We now propose to examine such evidence as we possess of the efficacy of lightning rods, whether they have met all the conditions required for perfect security against discharges of atmospheric electricity, without endangering the buildings to which they are applied, and finally to inquire into the validity of certain popular objections to their general employment.

It may be perceived, that in all these researches we have adhered carefully to the safe and beaten path of inductive science: in no case has any advance unwarranted by facts been attempted. The same caution will be observed in examining the different views which have been entertained of the efficacy and action of lightning rods. For, as it has been beautifully remarked by Lord Bacon, the great father of inductive science, "Man, who is the servant and interpreter of nature, can act and understand no further, than he has either in operation or in contemplation observed of the method and order of nature."

Whether Lightning Rods and other Metallic Conductors have effectually guarded Buildings, &c. against Damage by Lightning.

The cases in which continuous metallic conductors have afforded complete protection from lightning, are by no means few or inconclusive. We shall proceed to detail some of the most remarkable of such instances. Between the years 1820 and 1830 several church towers in Devonshire were struck by lightning: amongst these were Shaugh church, on the southern border of Dartmoor; Alphington church, near Exeter; Marlborough and Kingsbridge churches, on the southern coast; and Charles church, at Plymouth: of these, one only was protected by a lightning rod, viz., the church at Plymouth. Now it is an important fact, that although the conductor was broken in pieces by the shock, as already stated (p. 100), this was the only instance in which the church and tower escaped damage.

The church of St. Michael at Charlestown, was very frequently struck and damaged by lightning previously to the year 1760, when a lightning rod was applied to it. It has never suffered since.*

The Dutch church at New-York was struck by lightning in the year 1750, and again in 1763. The electrical discharge in each case passed over the metallic connections between the hammer of the bell and the works of the clock,—as in the cases of Brixton and St. Martin's churches, already mentioned (p. 100); in both instances portions of these connecting wires were melted, and the building was damaged.

In 1765, an iron rod was applied from the stem of the weathercock along the exterior of the building, and continued to the ground. During this year there again fell on it a heavy stroke of lightning: the building, however, was not in the least degree damaged, nor was any effect observable on the wire connecting the bell with the clock.†

The chapel of the château of the Count Orsini, in the province of Carinthia in Hungary, being on an elevated site, received such frequent damage from lightning, that divine service was no longer celebrated there. In the year 1730 a single discharge occurred, which at once laid the bell-tower in ruins. In 1778 the building was again nearly

* *Phil. Trans.*, vol. lxiv. p. 133.
† *Annuaire* for 1838, p. 604.

demolished by a similar explosion, and was again rebuilt. The great discovery of Franklin, however, began now to be appreciated, and a pointed lightning rod was applied to the tower. During the next five years, it was only once assailed by lightning, and then no damage ensued; nor does the building appear to have suffered since.*

The royal château at Turin was frequently damaged by lightning up to the year 1772, when Beccaria applied lightning rods to its principal roofs. Since that time, although frequently menaced by thunderstorms, it has remained uninjured.†

The fine tower of St. Mark, at Venice, more than three hundred and forty feet high, was repeatedly damaged by lightning, to which from its elevated position, it was greatly exposed. This tower terminates in a pyramid eighty-seven feet high, on which stands a wooden figure of an angel covered with copper. The detached pieces of iron employed in its construction produced (as at St. Bride's church in London) (p. 86) very destructive effects. It was damaged severely in 1388, at which time it was a wooden structure. In 1417 it was set on fire by lightning, and destroyed. In 1489 it was again struck, and the pyramid reduced to ashes. It was now rebuilt with stone. In the years 1548, 1565, and 1653, it again suffered from the same cause, and in 1745 a stroke of lightning fell on it with such

* Rozier, xxiv. p. 323.

† *Annuaire*, p. 605; Marbuch, *Enkyk. der Exp. Physik.* vol. i. p. 314.

tremendous force, that the whole tower was nearly ruined: it was rent in no less than thirty-seven places. The cost of repairs in this instance amounted to eight thousand ducats. In the years 1761 and 1762 it was again severely damaged.*

We have here sufficient evidence of the frequent effects of lightning on this building, whilst unprotected by a conductor. Now, in the year 1766, a lightning rod was applied along the exterior of the tower, reaching from the metallic figure on the top of the pyramid to the ground. Since this period we find no further account of its having suffered in the least degree from the effects of lightning.

We have already noticed the application of a lightning rod to the beautiful tower of the cathedral at Sienna (p. 92), which, although frequently struck and damaged by lightning before the application of the rod, has not since experienced any ill consequences, although struck by lightning in a similar way.

In ROZIER'S *Journal*, vol. xxii., we find an interesting and circumstantial account of a powder magazine at Glogau in Silesia, struck by lightning in May, 1782, and defended by a pointed lightning rod. "The flash was seen to leave the cloud and strike upon the rod; it appeared to envelope the whole building in electrical fire. The sentinel on guard lost his senses for some minutes, but no dam-

* Extract from registers of the city; ARAGO, *Annuaire* pour 1838.

age ensued." The conductor terminated in a well of water.

It may be well to contrast this result with the results in other cases, in which discharges of lightning have fallen in a similar way on magazines of gunpowder, not provided with lightning rods.

In March, 1782, about the same period, a discharge of lightning fell on a magazine at Fort Marlborough, in Sumatra, not having a lightning rod, and set fire to four hundred barrels of gunpowder.*

The magazine in the vaults of the church of St. Nazaire at Brescia, a large dépôt of gunpowder belonging to the republic of Venice, shared a similar fate, in August, 1769. The electrical discharge struck the tower, and descending to the vaults, exploded above 207,600 pounds of gunpowder.† By this dreadful catastrophe above three thousand persons perished, and nearly one-sixth of the beautiful city of Brescia was destroyed.

A similar accident occurred to a magazine at Malaga, in August, 1780, and at Tangiers, in May, 1785. At Luxembourg, in June, 1807, a magazine of gunpowder, built in former times by the Spaniards on a solid rock, was struck by lightning and blown up: more than 28,000 pounds, or about twelve tons of gunpowder, were fired, by which the lower part of the town was laid in ruins.‡

* MARSDEN'S *History of Sumatra*, third edition, p. 19.

† ARAGO, *Annuaire*, 1838, p. 483.

‡ Idem.

In September, 1808, a magazine near Venice was exploded by lightning, and in November, 1829, another at Navarino.* In the East Indies there have been very lately two explosions of this kind, viz., a magazine at Dum Dum, and a corning-house at Mazagon: both these establishments were unprovided with lightning rods.

Now it is to be observed, on the contrary, that although such rods have been employed for the defence of these buildings from lightning for more than seventy years, yet in no instance in which a lightning rod has been applied, has any explosion happened.

The protecting effect of a lightning conductor was well shown at Philadelphia, United States, in July, 1770: a severe thunderstorm overspread the city, and produced electrical discharges in four places, so that three houses and a merchant ship in the river were struck by violent detonations. One of the houses had a pointed lightning rod, and escaped damage: the other houses, on the contrary, together with the merchant ship, suffered considerably. On examining the point of the conductor on which the lightning fell, it was found to have been melted.†

The old church of St. Paul's, in London, not having been provided with a lightning rod, was twice struck by lightning and damaged. The pre-

* Report by Admiral Rosamel to the Minister of Marine, November, 1829.

† *Annuaire*, p. 609.

sent still more elevated building having lightning conductors of great magnitude, has never suffered from this source of danger.*

In addition to these instances of the operation of pointed metallic rods, in defending buildings against damage by lightning, it may be observed, that edifices furnished with continuous metallic masses, either with a view to utility or ornament, have seldom if ever suffered from atmospheric electricity.

The learned orientalist, Michaelis, states, that the temple of Jerusalem had not, during ten centuries, experienced a single condensed electrical explosion. Now, in examining the accounts given of this building, it appears to have been covered inside and out with burnished plates of metal,—Josephus says gold. The top was covered with a thick gilding, and bristled with long pointed iron or steel pikes. The object of this appears to have been to prevent birds from settling on the gilded dome. Under the court of the temple were cisterns, which received the rain from the roof through metallic pipes. A more complete system of efficient conductors of lightning could not have been devised. The conditions we have insisted on (p. 90), viz., that of bringing the building as nearly as possible into the same electrical position that it would be in, were it a complete metallic mass, are here fully satisfied, and we accordingly find, that this building never sustained

* *Phil. Trans.*

the slightest damage from lightning, although from its elevated position it was exposed to the frequent and terrible storms of Palestine. It is more than probable, from the circumstance of the roof having been covered with cedar, both within and without, that a heavy stroke of lightning falling on it, would, but for the metallic coatings, have set it on fire. When we consider (as observed by Arago), how carefully the ancients recorded instances of damage done to their buildings by lightning, it is impossible to explain the silence of historians on this point, except by admitting that the Jewish temple had never suffered in thunderstorms.

A parallel instance is found in the case of the cathedral at Geneva. This building, the most prominent and elevated in the whole city, has for more than two centuries enjoyed a perfect immunity from the effects of lightning, whilst the bell-tower of St. Gervais, situated much lower than the cathedral, has been frequently struck and damaged.

In the year 1771, Saussure investigated the cause of this, and on examination found, that the great central tower of the cathedral, built of wood, and which had existed above three hundred years, was completely covered from its summit with tinned iron plate: this communicated at the base of the tower with the various metallic masses about the roofs, and lastly by metallic pipes with the ground, thus forming an extensive and complete series of conductors, equivalent to the transmission of the most powerful electrical discharges.

The Monument near London Bridge, which by its construction has an uninterrupted series of conductors reaching through its interior, from the urn on its summit to the earth, is another instance. This building has remained safe amidst the many furious thunderstorms which have, since its erection in 1677, frequently spread over the metropolis, and damaged some of its principal edifices.

It may be observed as a general truth, that buildings in any way cased or supplied with metallic substances continued to the ground, invariably escape damage from lightning; and that where such metallic coverings or connections are only partially applied, the damage commences where they cease, and on the contrary, ceases where they commence. Thus one of the large granite chimneys, above a hundred feet high, at the Royal Victualling Yard, near Plymouth, was, on the 25th of May, 1841, rent by lightning sixty feet down, as far as the copper roofing of the building in connection with it: here all damage ceased, the copper having free conducting communication with the earth by the metallic pipes for carrying off the rain.

The effects of lightning on St. Peter's church in London, in the summer of the year 1774, are most remarkably conclusive on this point. The spire of this church was surmounted by a large key of gilded copper, and was covered with lead as far as the brick tower; accordingly so far no damage ensued, but between this and the leaded roof of the church the tower was much rent. At the roof, the metallic conduction again commenced, and continued to the ground; and here again the damage ceased.*

Such are some of the most striking facts bearing on the protective operation of lightning rods on buildings: we will now proceed to examine their influence on shipping.

In the year 1839 the Lords Commissioners of the Admiralty appointed a naval commission to investigate the best method of applying lightning conductors to Her Majesty's ships. After a very elaborate inquiry, they drew up a report on this important question, extending to more than eighty folio pages, and containing a valuable mass of oral and documentary evidence, received from naval officers, men of science, and other competent persons. This report was laid on the table of the House of Commons, and in February 1840 was ordered to be printed. One of the points to which the commission directed its attention was this: "Whether in a case in which ships *not having* lightning conductors have been struck by lightning, it appears that other ships in company *having* lightning conductors, have either not been struck, or have escaped injury." The following are some of the cases which were brought under the notice of the Commissioners:—

In 1815 His Majesty's ship *Norge*, was severely damaged by lightning, whilst the *Warrior*, of seventy-four guns, with a pointed conductor, lying close to the *Norge*, received no injury. The electrical ac-

* *Phil. Trans.*, vol. lxiv., p. 133.

tion in this case illuminated the linked portions of the conductor, and appeared to stream down into the sea. There were many other ships in the harbor, but none received any damage except one, *and this ship was the only one which had no conductor.*

In February, 1824, His Majesty's ship *Milford*, not having a lightning conductor, was struck by lightning in the Hamoaze, Devonport, and damaged, whilst His Majesty's ship *Caledonia*, of one hundred and twenty guns, about eighty fathoms distant, having pointed conductors, escaped.

In September, 1824, His Majesty's ships *Phaëton* and *Adventure* were lying at Gibraltar Mole: the *Phaëton* had not conductors, but the *Adventure* had: the ships were within a cable's length of each other. Under these circumstances the *Phaëton* was struck and damaged by lightning; the *Adventure* escaped.

In January, 1830, His Majesty's ships *Madagascar*, *Ætna*, and *Mosquito*, were about to come to an anchor off Corfu. A violent thunderstorm arose, which struck and severely damaged the *Madagascar* and *Mosquito*, the ships without conductors: the *Ætna*, which had a conductor at the main, although struck by lightning repeatedly on this mast, escaped.

In 1837, the *Cochin* tank-vessel, in Trincomalee harbor, had her foremast shivered by lightning, whilst Her Majesty's ship *Winchester*, about two cables, length distant, escaped. The *Winchester* had a conductor, and the lightning was observed to stream down it; the tank-vessel, on the contrary, was undefended.

In November, 1837, the *Pelican*, of sixteen guns, without a conductor, was struck by lightning on the coast of Africa, and damaged; the *Waterwitch*, another of Her Majesty's ships, at anchor within a short distance, escaped.

In March, 1838, Her Majesty's ship *Ceylon*, in Malta harbor, was struck by lightning, which shivered the foremast; she had no conductor. Her Majesty's ships *Talavera* and *Bellerophon*, both furnished with lightning conductors, escaped, as did the sheers for masting ships, which were similarly armed. This instance is the more remarkable, from the fact that the *Ceylon*, as a receiving ship, had only a short pole above her foremast, whereas the other ships, being fully rigged, their masts extended above one hundred and fifty feet into the air.

"In addition to these instances," say the Commissioners, "we beg to call their Lordships' attention to the case of the New-York packet, laid before the Lord High Admiral in 1827, by the Navy Board. It appears that on her passage to Liverpool, in 1827, this ship was struck by lightning, and sustained considerable injury. The conductor was not up at the time; but the weather continuing stormy, it was got out, and triced up to the mast-head. The ship was a second time struck by a most severe stroke of electricity, which fused the chain, and passed into the water without doing further damage." (pp. 52, 105.)

The following are some additional cases conclusive of the efficacy of lightning rods as a defence against lightning, the ships having been fitted with pointed conductors fixed in all their masts :—

His Majesty's frigate *Dryad* was struck by lightning in a tornado on the coast of Africa, in 1830. Commander Turner says, " that the discharge fell on both the fore and mainmasts with a loud whizzing sound; the thunder was nearly simultaneous with the lightning, and the ship appeared enveloped in flames."

His Majesty's frigate *Druid*, at Rio Janeiro, in 1832, encountered awful lightning, which was "conducted safely down the conductors on the fore and mainmasts." *

His Majesty's ship *Asia*, in the Tagus, in 1831, was assailed by lightning during a squall, with heavy rain; the electrical explosion passed off safely upon the conductor on the mainmast.†

Her Majesty's frigate *Talbot*, in July, 1842, was struck by lightning soon after getting under weigh at Sheerness. The lightning was observed to fall immediately on the conductor when the cloud burst over the mainmast head.‡

The cases of the *Beagle* and *Actæon*, referred to in our second section—each receiving heavy electrical charges upon their conductors, without harm—furnish very complete and important evidence of the beneficial operation of pointed conductors.

Lieutenant Sulivan, who had witnessed the effects of lightning in shattering the mast of His Majesty's

* *Report of Commission*, p. 94.

† Witnessed by Mr. Sadler, the master of the ship.

‡ Reported to the Lords of the Admiralty.

ship *Thetis*, happened to be on duty at the time the electrical discharge fell on the *Beagle;* he states that, "when the clouds by which the ship was enveloped burst on the mast, the mast and ship appeared to be wrapped in a blaze of fire; the vessel trembled under the crash of the thunder, and a vibratory whizzing sound was heard along the conductors."

Lieutenant Bonham, and Mr. May, the carpenter, who were both on deck when the *Actæon* was assailed by lightning, describe very similar effects. The discharges occurred within a fearfully short distance of the ship, and the flashes were so vivid, that the observers were for a time deprived of sight. When the ship was struck, the lightning was observed to fall immediately on the conductor; the crash of the thunder was intense and simultaneous with the lightning. The cutlasses stowed around the mast rattled in their stand, and there was a loud whizzing sound upon the conductor, which appeared enveloped in electrical fire."*

These cases, which have much in common, are characterized by well-known phenomena of electrical action; they have occurred in various parts of the world, at different times, and have been reported on by persons in no way interested in perverting the facts; hence, no doubt can remain as to the decisive evidence they afford, of the protecting power of pointed conductors.

* Account by the master.

Whether Lightning Rods attract Lightning.

Amongst the objections made to the employment of lightning rods, there appears to have been none so popular, and at the same time so plausible, as this, viz., that by setting up pointed conductors, we invite lightning to our buildings, which otherwise would not fall on them; that should the quantity of electricity discharged be greater than the rod can carry off, the redundant quantity must necessarily act with destructive violence; and that since we can never know the quantity of electricity which may be accumulated in, and be discharged from, the clouds, it is not improbable but that any conductor which we can conveniently apply, may be too small for the safe conveyance of such a charge.

Although the advocates of these opinions have never adduced any substantial fact, or any known law of electricity, in support of them; although they have never, by any appeal to experience, shown that buildings armed with lightning rods have been struck by lightning more frequently than buildings not so armed, nor demonstrated any single instance in which an efficient lightning rod, properly applied, has failed to afford protection,—nevertheless such views have been commonly entertained: indeed so strenuously have they been insisted on, and that, too, by persons of education and influence, that the Governor-general and Council of the Honorable the East India Company were led to order the lightning rods to be removed from their powder-magazines and other public buildings, having in the year 1838 come to the conclusion, from certain representations of their scientific officers, that lightning rods were attended by more danger than advantage; in the teeth of which conclusion, a magazine at Dum Dum, and a corning-house at Mazagon, not having lightning rods, were struck by lightning and blown up.*

In a work on Canada, published so lately as the year 1829,† we find the following passage: "Science has every cause to dread the thunder rods of Franklin: they attract destruction, and houses are safer without than with them. Were they able to carry off the fluid they have the means of attracting, then there could be no danger, but this they are by no means able to do." Assertions such as these, appealing as they do to the fears of mankind, rather than to their dispassionate and sober judgment, have not altogether failed in obtaining that sort of temporary favour which so frequently attends a popular prejudice, promulgated without reason, and received without proof. Not only is the idea that a lightning rod invites lightning unsupported by any fact, but it is absolutely at variance with the whole course of experience.

The notion that a lightning rod is a positive evil, appears to have arisen entirely out of assump-

* Correspondence with the Honorable Board of Directors; Professor Daniell and Dr. O'Shaughnessy.

† *Three Years in Canada.* By F. McTaggart, Civil Engineer in the service of the British Government.

tions, and a partial consideration of facts. Thus in consequence of the track of a discharge of lightning being always determined through a certain line or lines, which upon the whole least resist its progress, it has often been found to fall in the direction of pointed metallic bodies, such as vanes, vane-spindles, iron bars, knives, &c. The instances in which these bodies seem to have determined the course of lightning have been carefully recorded, the phenomena being peculiarly striking and remarkable (p. 86); but on the other hand, no attention has been given to those instances in which lightning has altogether avoided such bodies, and passed in other directions. (p. 72.) Now it will be found, as we shall presently show, that the action of a pointed conductor is purely passive. It is rather the patient than the agent; and such conductors can no more be said to attract or invite a discharge of lightning, than a watercourse can be said to attract the water which flows through it at the time of heavy rain.

We have shown in a former section (p. 106), what quantity of metal is really sufficient for the perfect conduction of any quantity of lightning liable to be discharged in the most severe thunderstorms: therefore, to assume that any conductor which may be applied is not sufficiently capacious, is to reason against experience, and to resort to a species of argument quite foreign to the conditions of the case. It would be, as if we were to insist upon the danger of applying water pipes to buildings, under the assumption that we do not really know what quantity of rain may possibly fall from the clouds, and that hence the pipe may after all be too small to convey it.

In all these reasonings we should recollect, as already explained (p. 12), that the forces in operation are distributed over a great extent of surface, and that the point or points upon which lightning strikes, is dependent on some peculiar condition of the intervening air, and the amount of force in operation, —not on the mere presence of a metallic body projecting for a comparatively short distance into the atmosphere,—"that such bodies provoke the shaft of heaven is the suggestion of superstition, rather than of science."*

We shall now leave the theoretical discussion of this question, and direct attention to the facts themselves, and examine how far the evidence deducible from such facts is conclusive upon this important point.

During the thunderstorm which spread over the neighborhood of Plymouth, in May, 1841, the electrical discharge struck one of the high chimneys at the Victualling-Yard, as already mentioned (p. 126); it fell also on the topmast of the sheer-hulk off the Dock-Yard, about a mile and a half distant. Now the circumstances attendant on these discharges of lightning bear directly on the question before us. The chimney at the Victualling-Yard is a round

* LESLIE, *Edin. Phil. Magazine.*

column of granite, about one hundred and twenty feet high, attached to the bakehouse; it *has not a particle of metal in its construction; nor has it any projecting point.* It stands at a distance of about one hundred yards from a clock-tower in the same yard; which, on the contrary, *has* not only a metal vane, and cross-pieces of metal, indicating the four cardinal points, but its dome is covered with copper, and there is a large conductor continued partly within and partly without the tower, from the dome to the ground. In the sheer-hulk a very small metallic wire was led along the pole topmast, and connected with the large metallic chains attached to the mast and sheers: the height of this pole was comparatively low, and it was completely overtopped by the neighbouring spars of the line-of-battle ship *Cornwallis*, fully rigged, and fitted with conductors on each of her masts. Now when the disruptive discharges took place, they fell on the granite tower, which had not a single metallic substance in its construction, and on the low flagstaff pole of the sheer-hulk's mast, notwithstanding that the clock-tower near the chimney offered every possible "invitation to the discharge, and the great altitude of the line-of-battle ship's spars were in the most favorable position for "attracting" the electrical explosion. The chimney was rent for sixty feet; the flagstaff of the hulk's mast was slightly injured, and the small wire broken and fused; the lower mast and chains were uninjured.

On the 25th of March, 1840, Her Majesty's ships

Powerful and *Asia*, each of eighty-four guns, were anchor within a short distance of each other in Vourla Bay, in the Mediterranean. The *Asia* had the fixed pointed conductors attached to each of her masts; the *Powerful* was unprovided with any lightning conductor whatever. Under these conditions they were both exposed to a severe thunderstorm. A discharge of lightning fell on the *Powerful*, the ship without conductors, and shivered some of her spars; whilst the *Asia*, where every supposed "invitation" to the discharge was most prominent, experienced no ill effect.

If no other cases were on record, these alone, would be sufficient to dispel all apprehensions of a metallic conductor "attracting or inviting" lightning. A great number of instances, however, equally clear and satisfactory, exist; from these we have selected the following:—

Amongst some interesting remarks on the effects of lightning, by Professor Winthrop, communicated by Dr. Franklin to Mr. Henley, it is stated, that a tree which stood at the distance of fifty-two feet only from a pointed conductor attached to a house, was struck by lightning and shivered, while the conductor and house escaped,*—that is to say, the lightning fell on a body, which, according to the prevalent notion, had little or no attraction for it, and held out no "invitation," in preference to one which did,—a fact totally at variance with the whole assumption.

* *Phil. Trans.* vol. lxiv., p. 152.

We have already adverted to the case of the *Southampton* (p. 72), in which a heavy electrical discharge fell upon the sea close to the ship, during a thunderstom on the east coast of Africa. But what makes this case especially applicable to the question now under consideration, is the circumstance, that all her masts were fitted with fixed lightning conductors, which terminated in copper spikes. The storm was awful, and it is stated by Mr. Martin, the master, to have lasted from ten P.M. to two A.M. "The night was pitchy dark, from the density of the surrounding clouds: the roar of the thunder was incessant, and the flashes of lightning frequently so vivid, as to affect the sight for some minutes," yet no ill effect was experienced; the electrical discharge was not drawn down in an explosive form exclusively upon the conductors, although it actually fell with violence upon the sea close to the vessel.

Similar effects were observed in His Majesty's ship *Sapphire*, armed with pointed conductors of the same kind. Captain Wellesley, who commanded this ship, states that "the lightning was so vivid, and the flashes so quick in succession all around the ship, that although the duty to be done was important, I hesitated to expose the crew to them;* yet the ship was not struck." In another place he states, "that the *Sapphire* often met with very severe lightning, but it was never attracted to her."†

The frequent instances in which lightning avoids

* They were afraid to hoist the boats out.

† *Report of Commission on Shipwreck by Lightning.*

the most prominent parts of of buildings, and falls obliquely upon some point far removed from them, may be further adduced as evidence against the attractive influence of such projections. The long zigzag track of lightning, arising from the resistance of the air to its more direct path, may cause it to fall very obliquely on the earth's surface, as is well known: indeed some of the directions of the zigzag, may become almost horizontal. Now, in these cases, the pointed extremities of a tower, or the masts of ships, have no influence whatever on the course of the explosion; which, on the principles already explained (p. 70), finds its way through the least resisting interval. Mr. Alexander Small states, in a letter to Dr. Franklin, that he saw an explosion of lightning pass before his window in a direction nearly horizontal, and strike a clock-tower far beneath its summit.

In the discharge of lightning, which fell on His Majesty's ship *Opossum* in the English Channel in March, 1825, "a peal of thunder burst on the main rigging, and split the topmast cap."* Her Majesty's ship *Pique* was struck by lightning in the St. Lawrence, in November, 1839, by a discharge which fell on the foremast just beneath the head of it, and from thence passing down the mast, did considerable damage. Such cases, although comparatively rare, and to a certain extent exceptions to the general course of lightning, are still sufficient to show how

* Ship's log.

little the direction of electrical explosions is determined by the influence of points *considered as mere attractors*, and that it is only when they can contribute to the equalization of the opposite electrical forces, that lightning strikes on them. Franklin, in endeavoring to draw off the electricity of a charged sphere by means of a pointed wire, found that the point when placed on a rod of glass or wax, had no action on it.*

When this large mass of evidence is duly considered, together with the fact, that lightning strikes indiscriminately, trees, rocks, and buildings, and even the ground near them, we are compelled to admit that properly constructed lightning rods are perfectly precise in their operation, and that the common notion that they "invite destruction" to our buildings, is not warranted by any sound argument drawn from experience.

It may not be unimportant to notice here the following extract from the *Memoirs of the Count de Forbin*, already alluded to. (p. 21.) In describing the large St. Helmo's fires, observed in the vane of the mainmast, he says, "I ordered one of the sailors to take it (the vane) down; but scarcely had he taken the vane from its place, when the fire fixed itself on the head of the mainmast, from which it was impossible to remove it;"† so that the presence of the metallic point was not at all necessary to the electrical discharge.

* FRANKLIN'S *Letters*, p. 56.

† *Letters on Electricity.* By the Abbé Nollet.—Vide *Phil. Trans.* for 1753, p. 201.

Before quitting the subject of the absolute protection from lightning afforded by conductors, the Naval Commission inquire, whether, according to the common prejudice, conductors have the power of *attracting* a flash of lightning, which in their absence would not have occurred; and their report states "that the instances of accidents to ships *without conductors*, and the comparatively rare occurrence of lightning being observed to *strike* on a conductor, would tend to negative such a supposition."* They further consider, from the instances which were submitted to them, of ships without conductors having been struck with lightning, in the presence of ships furnished with them, which were not so struck, that most complete evidence is afforded "either of the little influence exerted by such conductors in inducing or attracting an explosive discharge, or of their efficacy in harmlessly and imperceptibly conveying away electricity to the water."†

Whether in certain cases pointed Conductors actually prevent Explosions of Lightning from falling on Buildings. The Phenomena observed when a concentrated Discharge strikes upon a Conductor.

Coulomb proved by actual experiment, that the depth of the electric fluid on a conductor, always increases in a rapid proportion in approaching the

* *Report of Commission*, p. 4. † Idem.

edges; and that the effect is still more augmented at corners, which may be regarded as two edges combined. The effect is still further increased if any part of a conductor have the form of a point. Now the pressure of the air is probably the only force which retains the electric fluid on a conductor; and it is evident that if at the edges, corners, or angular points of a conductor, the electric depth be so much increased that the force of the electric fluid shall exceed the restraining pressure of the atmosphere, the electricity must escape. Accordingly, it is found practically impossible to accumulate any quantity of electricity on a conductor furnished with points.*

To discharge a Leyden phial silently. When a large jar is fully charged, which would give a violent shock, put one of your hands in contact with its outside coating, and with the other hand hold a sharp-pointed needle; and keeping the point directed towards the knob of the jar, proceed gradually towards it, until the point of the needle touches the knob. This operation discharges the jar completely, and the operator will either receive no shock at all, or so small a one as can hardly be perceived. The point of the needle, therefore, has silently and gradually drawn all the charge from the inside of the Leyden phial.

If this experiment be performed in the dark, the point of the needle will appear illuminated in its way toward the knob of the phial, which is another proof of its drawing off the charge.†

* *Noad's Electricity*, p. 13. † *Rees' Encyc.* vol. 13.

The Electrified Cotton. Take a small lock of cotton (*c*), extend it in every direction as much as may be practicable, and by means of a linen thread about

Fig. 14.

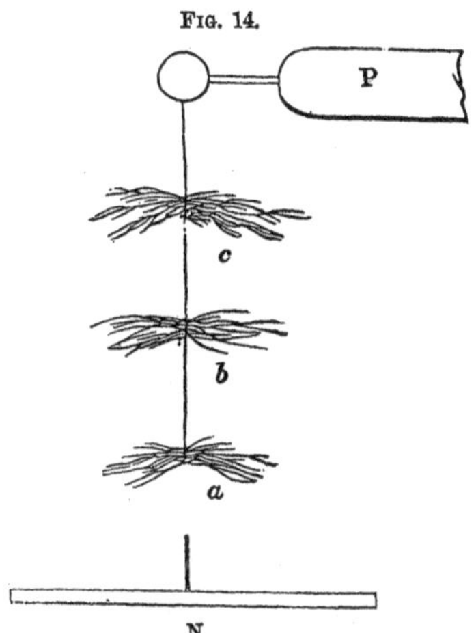

five or six inches long, or by a thread drawn out of the same cotton, tie it to the end of the prime conductor P; under this, attach in a similar way another lock (*b*), and to this a third lock (*a*); and then let the electrical machine be put in action, and the locks of cotton on being electrified, will immediately swell out, by repelling their filaments from each other, and will stretch themselves towards the nearest conductor. In this situation, the machine continuing in action, present the end of a finger or the knob of a wire, toward the lower lock of cotton, and this will then immediately move towards the finger, or the point N, endeavoring to touch it, much in the same way that the petty fragments on the lower surface of a thundercloud lean toward the earth. On presenting a needle at N. to the lowest lock, *a*, it immediately shrunk back upon the lock *b*, and this again upon *c*, and all together upon the conductor P, where the locks remained as long as the needle continued under them. Remove the needle, and the cotton will come again toward the finger. Present the needle, and the cotton will shrink again; which clearly shows that the needle, being sharp-pointed, draws off the electric fluid from from the cotton, and puts it in a state of being attracted by the prime conductor; which effort cannot be produced by a wire having a blunted end, or a round ball for its termination.

Dr. Franklin observes, "that electricity is not more disposed to leave, or more easily drawn off from any one part of an electrified sphere than from another. But that is not true of any other figure. From a cube it is more easily drawn at the corners than at the plane side, and so from the angles of a body of any other form, and still more easily from the angle that is the most acute. For the reasons, why electrified bodies discharge their electricity upon unelectrified bodies more easily, and at a greater distance from their angles and points than from their smooth sides, may not be easily determined. Different philosophers have advanced different theories; but of the nature of points all are agreed.

"Those points will also discharge into the air,

when the body is overcharged, without bringing any non-electric near to receive what is thrown off. For the air, though an electric *per se*, yet has always more or less water and other non-electric matters mixed with it; and these attract and receive what is so discharged.

"But points have a property, by which they *draw on* as well as *throw off* the electric fluid at greater distances than blunt bodies can. That is, as the pointed part of an electrified body will discharge the electricity of that body, or communicate it farthest to another body, so the point of an unelectrified body will draw off the electrical fluid from an electrified body, farther than a blunter part of the same unelectrified body will do. Thus a pin held by the head, and the point presented to an electrified body, will draw off its electricity at a foot distance; when, if the head were presented instead of the point, no such effect would follow. To understand this, we may consider, that if a person standing on the floor would draw off the electrical fluid from an electrified body, an iron crow and a blunt knitting-needle held alternately in his hand, and presented for that purpose, do not draw with different forces in proportion to their different masses. For the man, and what he holds in his hand, be it large or small, are connected with the common mass of unelectrified matter; and the force with which he draws is the same in both cases, it consisting in the different proportion of electricity in the electrified body and that common mass. But the force with which the electrified body retains its electricity by attracting it, is proportioned to the surface over which the particles are placed; *i. e.* four square inches of that surface retain their electricity with four times the force that one square inch retains its electricity. And as in plucking the hairs from the horse's tail, a degree of strength not sufficient to pull away a handful at once, could yet easily strip hair by hair; so a blunt body presented cannot draw off a number of particles at once; but a pointed one, with no greater force, takes them away easily, particle by particle.

"These explanations of the power and operation of points, when they first occurred to me, and while they first floated in my mind, appeared perfectly satisfactory; but now I have wrote them, and considered them more closely in black and white, I must own I have some doubts about them; yet, as I have at present nothing better to offer in their stead, I do not cross them out: for even a bad solution read, and its faults discovered, has often given rise to a good one, in the mind of an ingenious reader.

"Nor is it of much importance to us to know the manner in which nature executes her laws; 'tis enough if we know the laws themselves. 'Tis of real use to know that china left in the air unsupported will fall and break; but *how* it comes to fall, and *why* it breaks, are matters of speculation. 'Tis a pleasure indeed to know them, but we can preserve our china without it.

"Thus in the present case, to know this power of points may possibly be of some use to mankind, though we should never be able to explain it. The following experiments, as well as those in my first paper, show this power. I have a large prime conductor, made of several thin sheets of clothier's pasteboard, formed into a tube, near ten feet long and a foot diameter. It is covered with *Dutch* embossed paper, almost totally gilt. This large metallic surface supports a much greater electrical atmosphere than a rod of iron of fifty times the weight would do. It is suspended by silk lines, and when charged, will strike at near two inches distance a pretty hard stroke, so as to make one's knuckle ache. Let a person standing on the floor present the point of a needle at twelve or more inches distance from it, and while the needle is so presented, the conductor cannot be charged, the point drawing off the fire as fast as it is thrown on by the electrical globe. Let it be charged, and then present the point at the same distance and it will suddenly be discharged. In the dark you may see a light on the point when the experiment is made. And if the person holding the point stands upon wax, he will be electrified by receiving the fire at that distance. Attempt to draw off the electricity with a blunt body, as a bolt of iron round at the end and smooth (a silversmith's iron punch, inch thick, is what I use), and you must bring it within the distance of three inches before you can do it, and then it is done with a stroke and crack. As the pasteboard tube hangs loose on silk lines, when you approach it with the punch iron, it likewise will move towards the punch, being attracted while it is charged; but if, at the same instant, a point be presented as before, it retires again, for the point discharges it. Take a pair of large brass scales, of two or more feet beam, the cords of the scales being silk. Suspend the beam by a packthread from the ceiling, so that the bottom of the scales may be about a foot from the floor. The scales will move round in a circle by the untwisting of the packthread. Set the iron punch on the end upon the floor, in such a place as that the scales may pass over it in making their circle. Then electrify one scale, by applying the wire of a charged phial to it. As they move round you see the scale draw nearer to the floor, and tip more when it comes over the punch; and if that be placed at a proper distance, the scale will snap and discharge its fire into it. But if a needle be stuck on the end of the punch, its point upwards, the scale instead of drawing nigh to the punch and snapping, discharges its fire silently through the point and rises higher from the punch. Nay, even if the needle be placed upon the floor near the punch, its point upwards, the end of the punch, though so much higher than the needle, will not attract the scale and receive its fire, for the needle will get it and convey it away, before it comes nigh enough for the punch to act. And this is constantly observable in these experiments, that the greater quantity of electricity on the pasteboard tube, the farther it strikes or discharges its fire, and the point likewise will draw it off at a still greater distance. The same experiment slightly varied, is given by Mr. Harris: *c p b*,

Fig. 17, is a long bent arm of light brass wire balanced by means of central point *p* on the charging-rod of the jar J, and on which it has free motion in all directions; A is a light disc of gilded wood, resembling a common scale-pan, covered with a lock of fine cotton wool, and suspended by conducting threads

Fig. 17.

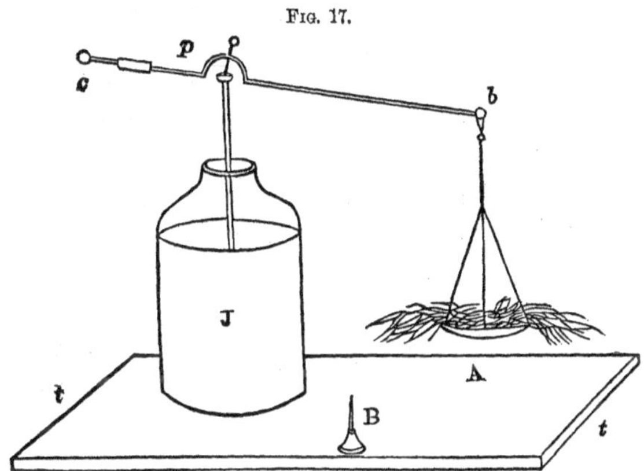

from the arm *c b p*. A pointed body B is placed on the same conducting base *t t* with the jar. If the jar be now charged, the cotton in the scale-pan will begin to extend its filaments, and the whole will be attracted toward the table, much in the same way as a cloud appears to be attracted toward the earth, causing the bent arm *c p b* to assume an inclined position. If the arm be now caused to move upon its centre *p*, so as to allow the artificial cloud A to approach the point B, the arm will gradually assume its previous horizontal position, in consequence of the influence of the point in neutralizing the opposite forces. As the artificial cloud continues to approach the point, this action proceeds so rapidly, as frequently to produce a whizzing sound, the bent arm recovering at the same time its horizontal position; the scale-pan A, so far from being attracted by the point, actually recedes from it, and very faithfully represents the kind of operation of pointed bodies on charged clouds, viz., their power of discharging the electricity of the clouds without attracting them.

"When the distances and charge are nicely adjusted, this experiment is very striking and satisfactory.

"Now if the fire of electricity and that of lightning be the same, as I have endeavored to show at large, in a former paper, this pasteboard tube and these scales may represent electrified clouds. If a tube of only ten feet long will strike and discharge its fire on the punch at two or three inches distance, an electrified cloud of perhaps 10,000 acres may strike and discharge on the earth at a proportionably greater distance. The horizontal motion of the scales over the floor, may represent the motion of the clouds over the earth; and the erect iron punch, a hill or high building; and then we have electrified clouds passing over hills or high buildings at too great a height to strike, which may be attracted lower till within their striking distance. And lastly, if a needle fixed on the punch with its point upright, or even on the floor below the punch, will draw the fire from the scale silently at a much greater than the striking distance, and so prevent its descending towards the punch; or if in its course it would come nigh to strike, yet being first deprived of its fire it cannot, and the punch is thereby secured from the stroke; I say, if these things are so, may not the knowledge of this power of points be of use to mankind, in preserving houses, churches, ships, &c., from the stroke of lightning?"

Mr. Wilcke, who made some very acute remarks on Franklin's views of electricity, states, that he witnessed the result of this action of pointed bodies on the great scale of nature, in August, 1758. A large fringed cloud, strongly electrified, and extending its inferior surface towards the earth, suddenly lost its electrical character, in passing over a forest of tall fir trees. The ragged and depending portions shrank back upon the main cloud, and rose up, as it were, from the earth.*

The great number of cases we have cited (pp. 118, 132), with a view of showing, not only the protecting effect of lightning rods, but their passive character as attractors of lightning, may be further adduced, in illustration of this peculiar property of pointed conductors. Indeed, it is almost impossible to account for the fact of so many buildings being repeatedly struck by lightning, before they were furnished with lightning rods, and so seldom struck afterwards, and that lightning has seldom, if ever, been observed

* FRANKLIN'S Letters, p. 351.

to fall in an explosive form upon buildings involving pointed metallic conductors in their construction,—without admitting that the conductors had rapidly neutralized the electrical state of the air, and so prevented the occurrence of a dense explosion.

We find this effect especially apparent (p. 118) in the case of the tower of St. Mark at Venice, the chapel of the Count Orsini, the temple of Jerusalem, the monument of London, the cathedral at Geneva, and many others; and if we add to these the remarkable instances of certain ships of the British navy, enveloped as it were in violent thunderstorms in tropical climates, without any dense explosion falling on them, the evidence of this action of pointed conductors, in mitigating the fury of electrical discharges, is as complete as any evidence from experience can be imagined.

We have deemed it worth while to thus extend illustrations of the power of points to draw on, and to throw off the electrical fluid, on account of the intrinsic practical importance of the subject to the community, who have churches and other public buildings to protect, and to private citizens, who have lives, houses, and various kinds of property exposed. For, without a due appreciation of this power of points, no intelligent conviction can be had as to the proper construction of lightning conductors.

Phenomena observed when a dense Explosion of Electricity falls on a Lightning Rod.

Instances in which the forces have not been so rapidly neutralized by the action of pointed bodies, as to prevent some portion of the discharge from falling upon the conductor in a concentrated form, are by no means common: when they do occur, however, the explosive action subsides in striking on the point. The phenomena in such cases correspond accurately with those of artificial electricity, and are of a highly interesting character. The crash of the thunder is attended by a loud whizzing sound, described by some observers as the rushing of water, or like the sound heard on lifting the valve of a steam boiler; at the same time the conductor becomes covered with a luminous glow or streak of light, and appears at the part struck to be enveloped in electrical fire.

The luminous appearance was observed at an early period of the application of lightning rods. When the heavy discharge fell upon the tower at Sienna, in 1777, several persons noticed upon the conductor a long and regular train of light.* At the time of the dense electrical explosions which fell upon Her Majesty's ships *Druid*, *Beagle*, *Dryad*, &c. (p. 130), the observers all agree in representing the discharge as attended by a loud whizzing sound, and upon the conductors a transient glow of light.

These phenomena are easily produced by artificial means. If we attempt to discharge a highly charged jar through a pointed rod, a loud whizzing noise, in the direction of the point, will be heard,

* Tilloch's *Mag.*, viii., p. 318.

immediately before the dense explosion takes place. The production of the light is not so easily accounted for; but the results of scientific inquiry favor the opinion that it is a sort of glow, between metal and air immediately in the points of contact; that it is of a perfectly harmless nature, and may be classed with the phosphorescent flashes attendant on the aurora borealis, or with the streaming of ordinary electricity in the exhausted receiver of an air-pump. It may be produced artificially on a conducting wire, either by increasing the electrical charge, in respect of the size of the wire, or diminishing the atmospheric pressure.

Harmless Character of the Luminous Appearances observed on Lightning Rods.

It is essential to distinguish between this glow on the surface of lightning rods and the heat evolved by the passing shock. We have already shown (p. 109) that no mass of metal, equal in conducting power to a copper rod half an inch in diameter and two feet in length, has ever been fused or even sensibly heated by lightning;* and it is well known that any quantity of electricity may be discharged through a conducting rod, even whilst in contact with the most inflammable compounds, such as gunpowder, &c., without igniting them, provided the temperature of the rod be not considerably in-

* *Shipwreck by Lightning, Report and Evidence*, p. 13.

creased by the discharge. If the atmospheric pressure about such a wire be diminished, we immediately observe it covered, at the instant of the discharge, with a luminous glow, yet it is not sensibly heated, nor will inflammable matter in contact with it be inflamed.

There are many interesting examples on record, of the small degree of heat of this species of electrical action. The St. Helmo's fires, and other electrical lights which so often settle on the masts and ropes of ships, are unattended by any calorific effect; and persons during electrical storms, have appeared to be enveloped in weak flames, without being at the time in any way conscious of it.

A remarkable instance of the harmless nature of these appearances was observed by Ross and Sabine, in returning from their last Arctic expedition. In the Greenland seas, during a dark, cloudy night, they observed a sort of glow discharge on the surface of the water, directly in the ship's course. It appeared to occupy a space of four or five hundred yards, and had very considerable elevation. The vessel at length sailed out of a pitchy darkness, directly into this luminous mass; all at once the masts, yards, and sails, as the successive masts passed forward, became covered with light. The ship having sailed completely through it, became again involved in profound obscurity.*

* Communication from Dr. Robison to Mons. Arago.—*Annuaire* for 1838, p. 372.

This was evidently one of those glow discharges already explained (p. 38). The deep black clouds covering the sky being particularly indicative of that peculiar condition of the atmosphere observed in thunderstorms (p. 52); as evidence of the small heating effect of this species of electrical light, the result is very important and conclusive.

Division of the Charge.

Although there is no instance on record of an isolated lateral explosion of electricity from a lightning rod, yet we find instances in which the discharge has divided between the conductor, and other metallic bodies in connection with the earth.

Arago, in his valuable "*Notices sur le Tonnerre*," published in the *Annuaire* of 1838, has quoted an instructive case of this nature.* It appears that for the protection of a house in the United States of America, a lightning conductor had been applied on the outside of the building, similar to that represented in the annexed figure (16), in which P is a pointed bar of iron projecting from the roof, N, a similar bar driven into the ground, at P *t* a small brass wire connecting the bar. At the point *n*, inside the house, stood a fowling-piece, *n*, with its barrel against the wall, and separated from the conductor P N only by the thickness of the masonry. The consequence was, that when a discharge of

* FRANKLIN'S *Works*, vol i., p. 361.

lightning fell on the conductor at P, and passed on the small wire P *t*, it divided at the point *n*, upon the two circuits, and in doing this broke out a large

Fig. 16.

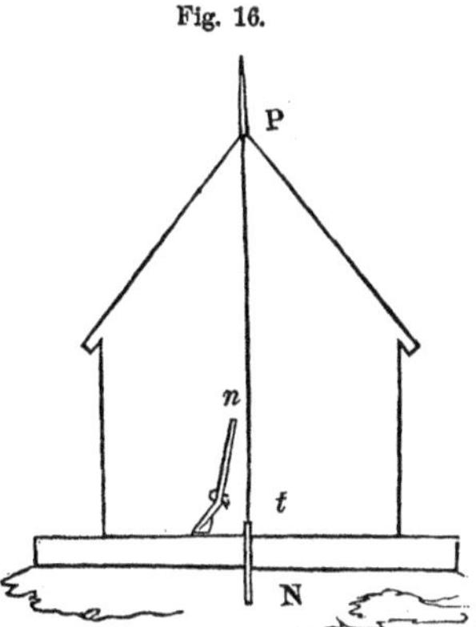

hole in the wall of the house, and shattered the stock of the gun in forcing a passage to the earth. The small wire P *t* was completely melted so far as the point *n*, but not beyond it; the resistance in the direction P *t* N, at the point of fusion of the wire, evidently exceeded or was equal to the resistance in the direction P *n* N; hence the metal in the fowling-piece evidently saved the remaining portion of the wire *n t*.

The cases quoted of the damage by lightning to the Hôtel des Invalides, at Paris (p. 101), to the French frigate *La Junon*, as also the shock experienced by the two sailors in the French frigate *La Calypso*, are all instances of this division of the charge between the conductor and other lines of transit to the earth or sea. It is quite clear, that in these cases the resistance to the progress of the discharge through the small and very long ropes of wire, exceeded, or was at least equal to, the resistance in other directions; consequently, these instances are very similar to the preceding.

"I am not aware," says Faraday, in speaking of such cases, "of any phenomenon called lateral discharge, which is not a diversion of the primary current;" "all liability to a division of the main charge would decrease in proportion to the capacity of the primary conductor."*

Instances in which Buildings provided with pointed Conductors are said to have been damaged by Lightning.

Although several instances have occurred in which buildings having pointed lightning rods have been damaged by lightning, yet it is a singular fact, that they may all be quoted in illustration of the great advantage of such rods, in safely transmitting heavy electrical discharges from the atmosphere.

We have shown, by reference to a variety of cases, both the small influence of pointed conductors in attracting or causing explosions of lightning, and the liability of the discharge to break up, before reaching the earth, into two or more streams

* *Report and Evidence on Shipwreck by Lightning*, pp. 34, 35.

(pp. 135, 136). In the cases of damage by lightning said to have occurred, notwithstanding the presence of a pointed conductor, the electrical discharge has divided in the air into two or more streams, previously to striking the building. One portion has commonly struck upon the conductor, and been carried off by it, whilst other portions have fallen on points far distant from the conductor.

The first instance claiming attention, is the case of the church of "Notre Dame de la Garde," at Genoa, struck and damaged by lightning on the 14th August, 1779, a lightning rod having been applied to it in the previous year.

The church stands on one of the highest hills in the neighborhood of Genoa, and clouds are constantly hanging over it; the bell tower to which the conductor had been applied, was originally even with the façade, but in consequence of a subsequent enlargement of the church, and the erection of a porch, it was thrown far back. The lightning conductor commenced from a stout iron rod, tipped with a gilded copper point; this rod projected from the top of the bell-tower three feet into the air, and from its termination a stout iron bar was continued, and led out through a window over the roof of the church, and so on to the ground. Before the lightning struck the church, it bifurcated (p. 36); one of the explosions fell on the conductor, split open the gilded copper point, and was conducted safely to the earth: the other explosion struck the porch at a distance from the conductor, descended into the church, and did some damage; several persons who were in a room over the porch felt a violent shock, many were thrown down, but not hurt.

This account has been obtained from the *Sammlungen zur Physik*, for 1782:* the writer states that the accident was attributed to the conductor, but he shows that if the conductor had not been there, much greater damage must have ensued, and thinks it is perfectly clear that the church was struck in two places,—first on the conductor; secondly, upon the unprotected porch. This case, therefore, does not furnish any argument against the employment of lightning rods, but rather shows their value, and points out the necessity of securing the portions of a building which are distant from the rod.

The case already alluded to (p. 111) of the Board-house at the Purfleet magazines having been struck by lightning, in May, 1777, is another instance in which a building furnished with a lightning rod was damaged. From the description of this building, it will be seen that the corner struck was forty-six feet distant from the point of the conductor. Little or no damage was done: a few stones only were displaced. Now, there can be very little doubt but that the conductor really carried off safely and silently a great portion of the discharge; it is impossible to explain on any other principle how so small an amount of damage ensued from so heavy a discharge as this appears to have been, especially if we suppose it to

* Vol. ii., p. 588.

have been concentrated upon two clamps on a corner of the building. The probability is, that the discharge bifurcated, as in the preceding case; and whilst one division rushed through the conductor, the other struck a distant point of the house. The clamps on which it fell, were fixed in the coping-stones of the parapet, and were about seven inches above the lead gutters of the roof, which constituted a portion of the general system of conduction to the ground.

The discharge, in forcing its way through seven inches of bad conducting matter to the lead beneath, did some damage by an intermediate explosion, but it was very inconsiderable; had the iron clamps been continued to the general mass of metal on the roof, it is quite certain that no damage whatever would have occurred.

In the account given of this case in the *Transactions of the Royal Society*, it appears that an observer who witnessed the descent of the lightning, saw it divide in some point, P (fig. 17), into "three fire-balls," as he termed them. One of these struck in the direction of the conductor at *c*, another damaged the corner of the building at *m*, together with a shed at *s*, and the third struck upon the ground in front of the house, near a gate, at G.*

This was evidently an instance of the trifurcation of lightning (p. 36), one of the divergent branches or streams having fallen on the conductor. But this

* *Phil. Trans.*, vol. lxxii., p. 377.

part of the explosion was discharged safely into the earth, whilst the shed *s*, and corner *m*, which were unprotected, suffered. This case, therefore, affords

Fig. 17.

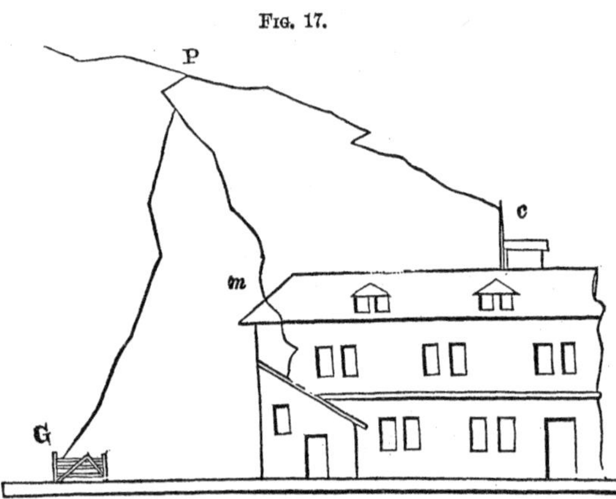

conclusive evidence of the value of lightning rods. The committee of the Royal Society, in a report on this circumstance, considered that the rods were not so "perfectly applied as they ought to have been;" they were, however, sufficiently well applied to meet any discharge of lightning likely to have fallen on them. No part of the building near them was damaged, and it is not to be expected that they should defend parts at a great distance, especially when such parts are the first exposed to an electrical cloud moving toward them, and likely to strike upon them obliquely (p. 135).

The instance in which lightning fell upon a magazine of powder at Bayonne, in February, 1829, furnishes another remarkable illustration of the liability of the electrical discharge to divide in the air, and strike on a part of a building distant from a lightning rod, as well as on the rod itself. This case, which was reported on by the physical section of the Royal Academy of Sciences at Paris, gave rise to much interesting discussion.

The building is about fifty-six feet in length, and about thirty-six feet wide: it is covered by thick vaulted masonry, and a sloping roof with gable ends: these were protected by plates of lead; the gutters also were of lead, and there were the usual appendages for discharging the rain.

The lightning rod projected about twenty feet above the building: it was attached to the lead of the roof by a metallic socket, through which it passed, and which was soldered to one of the lead coverings. Instead of being carried, however, directly into the earth at the foot of the wall, it was turned outward, at about two feet from the ground, and, being bent at right angles, was continued on semi-insulating posts of wood into a trench filled with charcoal, distant thirty-three feet from the wall.

On the 23d of February, 1827, about 4 A. M., a discharge of lightning fell on this building. The point of the conductor was melted, and the plates of lead, by which it was attached to the wood posts at the foot of the wall, were more or less torn and perforated by holes. No damage, however, ensued to the building in the course of the conductor. At the southwest corner, a sheet of lead covering the gable end was torn out immediately over a point where two stones of the cornice were united by an iron cramp. Hence, as in the case of the magazine at Purfleet, this distant part of the building was also visited by an electrical explosion.

The reporters state, that the conductor, in consequence of being continued at so great a distance from the building, did not offer a sufficiently easy line of transit for the discharge to the earth, which is, they think, evident, from the damage to the wooden posts on which the conductor was supported: hence they infer, that the discharge divided between the conductor on which it first struck, and the metals of the roof, and that the small rent on the lead, on the southwest angle, was the result of this division, in a point through which the electrical discharge found its way; that this is the more probable from the circumstance of the rain having at this point beaten against the walls, and so increased the facility of conduction by means of a "sheet of water, to the ground."*

The following well authenticated instances of recent occurrence, in which lightning has fallen upon bodies in the vicinity of conductors, as well as upon the conductor itself, are very similar to those just described, and they furnish satisfactory evidence of the nature of such cases.

Her Majesty's brig *Racer*, commanded by Captain J. Hope, was struck by lightning in May, 1835,

* *Annales de Chimie*, tome xl., p. 391.

in latitude 39° north, longitude 63° west; a chain conductor was up at the mainmast. The electrical discharge fell with destructive violence on the foretopgallant mast, distant from the conductor about forty feet, at the same time sparks were seen on the chain, and a rustling noise was heard throughout its length* (p. 131). We have here a remarkable illustration of the nature of the accident at Purfleet. The conductor evidently transmitted without explosion a great portion of the discharge, and consequently prevented the damage which must have ensued, had the whole been concentrated on a single unprotected point.

Dr. O'Shaughnessy relates the following instance of the bifurcation of lightning,† which, on examination, will be found to have a very forcible application to the case of the damage done to the magazine at Bayonne. It appears that, in May, 1837, an electrical explosion divided upon two adjoining houses in Chowringhee, East Indies; one of the houses not having a lightning rod, in the occupation of Dr. Goodeve, was struck and damaged, whilst the adjoining house, tenanted by Mr. Trower, and to which a lightning rod had been applied, escaped, although a portion of the explosion fell on it with great violence. "Dr. Goodeve, while walking in the verandah, saw the lightning strike Mr. Trower's conductor, and at the same time strike his own house." The

* Ship's log, with remarks by Captain J. Hope, R. N.

† Reports to the Honorable the Court of Directors of the East India Company.

distance of the damaged part of Dr. Goodeve's house from the conductor, appears, from a subsequent examination, to have been sixty-six feet, about the same distance as that in the case of the Heckingham poor-house, just described.

This case so remarkably conclusive as to the protecting effect of lightning rods, has nevertheless been adduced as an evidence of their liability to draw down greater discharges upon buildings than they can transmit, thus causing damage to surrounding bodies; we have, however, already shown (p. 136), that pointed metallic rods have no such attractive influence, and that discharges of lightning are determined towards the earth by very different causes. But even if it were true, that a pointed metallic rod did invite or attract lightning towards it, still we cannot suppose it to attract more than it can conduct, since the attraction would entirely depend on the superior conducting power of metals; to assert, therefore, that a conductor can draw towards it more lightning than it can conduct, is to assert in other words that it attracts more than it can attract, which is evidently an absurd proposition.

The last instance which Mr. Snow notices of damage done by lightning to a building furnished with a conductor, is the case of the Melville Monument, in St. Andrew's Square, Edinburgh. It consisted of a pointed metallic rod, which passed through the statue, and was connected with an iron chain led through a hollow way in the staircase to the ground.

On the 14th of July, 1837, an electrical explosion fell on this building, by which the wooden door leading from the staircase to the platform of the gallery was forced off its hinges, and the stones at the top near the door were loosened. On examining the conductor after the accident, it appeared that the chain connecting the pointed rod with the ground had been, by accident or design, drawn up for some considerable distance through the hollow way in the staircase, and coiled round a stick placed across the top of the stone tube round which the stair was built. The stick was so placed as to press against the door leading to the platform, in order to keep it shut.

The damage in this case, therefore, did not arise from any failure in the principle on which the conductor was applied, but entirely in consequence of the displacement of its inferior portion, which reduced it to the condition of a semi-insulated mass of metal.

A church in Connecticut, in which were assembled the congregation, was struck by lightning. Prof. Brocklesby, of Trinity College, Hartford, who related to the writer the circumstances, was in the house at the time of the explosion. The spire had a single round rod, running down to the ground. The charge was oblique, and came in a direction opposite to the spire, and struck the end of the church most remote from the steeple. But this instance cannot be adduced as evidence against the principle on which lightning conductors are applied, since, according to the known laws of electricity, the rod could render no protection whatever—the lightning not coming within its sphere of attraction.

The writer would add the case of Mr. Platt's house, in Deep River, Connecticut, already alluded to, under the head, "Ascending or Upward Stroke." This instance has often been adduced, as an argument against the efficiency of lightning conductors. But nothing could be more unfair. I know not who erected the two rods upon this house. A. M. Quinby, Esq., of this city, speaking of this instance through the public prints, asserts, "that they were Spratt's patent, put up by a Dr. Minor, of Hartford, Connecticut; but they were so improperly constructed and attached, that they could not be at all responsible for the harm suffered by the building." The disruptive charge being upward, and occurring on the front side of the house, and the rod running down only on the back side, the lightning had no chance of getting on to the rod, except by going clear round the house, or passing over the top. Evidently, in attempting the latter, the force of the charge passed into the building ere it could reach the rod. Hence the destruction which followed.

This instance is thus noticed in an editorial of the Saybrook Mirror, June 24, 1852:—

"*Singular Freak of Lightning.*—During the shower on Wednesday of last week, the house of A. J. Platt, of Deep River, was struck, doing considerable damage. It appeared to be what is called an *upward stroke*, passing up the door-casing of the hall-door, knocking off the plastering in the hall and parlor, and thence, through the hall, the side of the house, where the wing connects, to the corner of the wing, passing down on a pillar; and also at another point into the sink, knocking off splinters, and loosening the clapboards in various places.

"A singular feature is, that the house was guarded by a lightning rod attached to each chimney, running down the roof, and from thence to the ground; and there is abundant evidence that the electric current, in its progress, passed within some six or seven feet of this rod, and that the protection which it is claimed to give, was of no avail in this instance. The rod is one of those put up by Dr. Minor, who has also put up several in this village, and we would like to hear his explanation of their inefficiency in this case, as he claims them as superior to any other.

"That there is sure protection in a conductor, we believe, and it would be well for those about to procure this safeguard, to ascertain that they procure the best article, and have them rightly put up. It is a matter which is not lightly to be passed over, where the lives of people and property are at stake."

In so long a period as three-quarters of a century, it is not to be expected that no casualties should occur, either from a defective application of the conductor, or from an explosion falling on some part of the building at a distance from the conductor.

Precautions when exposed to the action of Thunderstorms.

From circumstances of almost constant inquiry attending thunderstorms, it is impossible to witness one without some feelings of personal danger; in this case attention to the following observations may often be of service in relieving the mind from unnecessary fear, or in suggesting the necessary steps to be taken for the prevention of accident.

The precautions generally offered by writers on electricity, as necessary for the safety of those who are exposed to the action of a thunderstorm, may be thus enumerated: "shelter should not be taken under trees, hedges, &c., for, should they be struck, such situations are particularly dangerous; at the same time a person is much safer at about thirty or forty feet from such objects than at a greater distance, as they are likely to operate as conductors. Large portions of water also ought to be carefully avoided if possible, and even streamlets that may result from recent rain; these are good conductors, and the height of a human being connected with them, may sometimes determine the course of the lightning. In a house the safest situation is considered to be the middle of the room; and this situation may be rendered still more secure by standing on a glass-legged stool; but, as such an article is not in the possession of many people, a hair mattress, or a thick woollen hearth-rug makes a very good substitute. It is very injudicious to take refuge, as some persons do, in the cellar during a thunderstorm, since the discharge is often found to be from the earth to the clouds, and many instances are recorded of buildings that were struck having sustained the greatest injury about the basement story. But, whatever situation is chosen, the greatest care should be taken to avoid going near the fire-place, since the chimneys are most likely to attract the fluid, and even if there be no fire in the grate, at the time, it should be remembered that soot is a powerful conductor. The same caution is necessary with respect to all large metallic surfaces; gilt furniture, bell wires, &c."*

Construction of Lightning Rods applied to Buildings.

But the most important and useful application that has ever yet been made of the discoveries of the electrician is in the method of securing buildings, ships, &c., from effects of lightning. To the ingenuity of Dr. Franklin the world is indebted for this invention, as well as for his discovery of the identity of lightning and common electricity; and these are justly considered two of the grandest discoveries of last century.

As this subject is of the utmost importance, we shall here quote the opinions of many of the most eminent electricians who have written on the subject of lightning conductors. Mr. Cavallo, speaking of the proposal of Dr. Franklin, which we have just

* *London Encyclopædia*, vol. 8, p. 59.

noticed, remarks "that the reasonableness and truth of such an assertion has been confirmed by numerous facts, and the practice of raising such conductors has been found exceedingly useful, particularly in hot climates, where thunderstorms are very frequent, and the damage occasioned by the same too often experienced.

"In regard to the construction of such conductors, there have been some controversies among electricians; and the most advantageous manner of using them has not, without a great many experiments, and but very lately, been ascertained." Some philosophers have asserted that such conductors should terminate in an obtuse end, that they might the less invite the lightning from the clouds; for such an end will not attract electricity from so great a distance as a sharp point. But other philosophers have thought a pointed termination to be much preferable to an obtuse one; and their assertion seems, on the following accounts, to be better founded.

"A sharp-pointed conductor, it is true, will attract electricity from a greater distance than one with an obtuse point, but at the same time will attract and conduct it very gradually, or rather by a continued stream, in which manner a remarkably small conductor is capable of conducting a very great quantity of electricity; whereas an obtusely terminated conductor attracts the electricity in a full separate body, or explosion, by which it is often made red hot, melted, and even exploded in smoke, and by such a quantity as perhaps would not have at all affected it, if it had been sharply pointed.

"A sharp-pointed conductor certainly invites the matter of lightning easier than an obtuse one; but to invite, receive, and conduct it in small quantities, never endangers the conductor; and the object of fixing a conductor to a house, is to protect the house from the effects of, and not the conductor from transmitting, the lightning.

"It is an observation much in favor of sharp-pointed conductors, that such steeples of churches, and edifices in general, as are terminated by pointed metallic ornaments, have very seldom been known to be struck by lightning; whereas others that have flat terminations and have a great quantity of metal in a manner insulated on the top, are often struck; and it is but seldom that they escape without great damage.

"Besides these considerations a sharp-pointed conductor, by the same property of attracting electricity more readily than an obtusely terminating one, may prevent a stroke of lightning, which the latter is incapable of doing.

"A conductor, therefore, to guard a building, should be fastened to the wall, not by iron cramps, but by pieces of wood. If this conductor were quite detached from the building, and supported by wooden posts the distance of one or two feet from the wall, it would be much better. The upper end of the conductor should be terminated in a pyramidal form, with the edges, as well as the point, very sharp; and if the conductor be of iron, it should be gilt. This sharp end should be elevated above the highest part of the building (as above a stack of chimneys, to which it may be fastened) at least five or six feet. The lower end should go five or six feet into the ground, and in a direction leading from the foundation; or it would be better to connect it with the nearest piece of water, if any be at hand. If this conductor, on account of the difficulty of adapting it to the form of the building, cannot conveniently be made of one rod, then care should be taken, that, where the pieces meet, they be made to come in as perfect a contact with one another as possible; for electricity finds considerable obstruction where the conductor is interrupted.

"In ships a chain has often been used for this purpose, which, on account of its pliableness, has been found very convenient, and easy to be managed among the rigging of the vessel; but as the electricity finds a great obstruction in going through the several links, so that chains have been actually broken by the lightning, their use is now almost entirely laid aside."

Mr. Cavallo gives with cordial approbation, the following extract from the Earl of Stanhope's learned work on electricity. As requisites for the proper construction of conducting rods for the preservation of buildings from the effects of lightning he directs, (1.) "That the rods be made of such substances as are the best conductors of electricity. (2.) That the rods be uninterrupted and perfectly continuous. (3.) That they be of sufficient thickness. (4.) That they be perfectly connected with the main rod. (5.) That the upper extremity of the rods be as acutely pointed as possible. (6.) That it be very finely tapered. (7.) That they be prominent. (8.) That each rod be carried in the shortest convenient direction, from the point at its upper end to the main rod. (9.) That there be neither large nor prominent bodies of metal upon the top of the building proposed to be secured, but such as are connected with the conductor by some proper metallic communication. (10.) That there be a sufficient number of high and pointed rods."

A very interesting report on the subject of lightning conductors, was presented to the Royal Academy of Sciences by M. Gay Lussac. The information contained in it may be regarded in many respects as the most perfect we possess on the subject. In this paper we learn "that the electric matter tends always to spread itself over conductors, and to assume a state of equilibrium in them, and becomes divided among them in proportion to their form and principally to their extent of surface; and that hence a body that is charged with the fluid being in communication with the immense surface of the earth, will retain no sensible portion of it."

Gay Lussac defines a lightning rod "to be a conductor which the electric matter prefers to the surrounding bodies, in order to reach the ground, and expand itself through it, and should descend without any divisions or breaks in its length into water or moist ground. When a conductor has any breaks in it, or is not in perfect communication with a moist soil, the lightning having struck it, flics from it to some neighboring body, or divides itself between the two, in order to pass more rapidly into the earth.

"The most advantageous form that can be given to the extremity of a conductor, is that of a sharp cone; and as iron is very liable to rust by the action of air and moisture, the point of the stem would soon become blunt; and therefore, to prevent it, a portion of the top should be composed of a conical stem of brass or copper, gilt at its extremity; and the higher it is elevated in the air, other circumstances being equal, the more its efficacy will be increased."

"The rod should be supported parallel to the roof, at about six inches distance from it, by forked stanchions; and after turning over the cornice of the building without touching it, should be brought down the wall. In a dry soil, or on a rock, the trench to receive the conductor should be at least twice as long as that for a common soil, and even longer, if thereby it be possible to reach moist ground. Should the situation not admit of the trench being much increased in length, others in a transverse direction should be made, in which the lower extremities of the conductor are to be placed. In general, the trench should be made in the dampest, and consequently, lowest spot, near the building, and the water gutters made to discharge their waters over it, so as to keep it always moist. Too great precaution cannot be taken to give the lightning a ready passport to the ground, for it is chiefly on this that the efficacy of a conductor depends."*

* *London Encyclopædia*, vol. viii., p. 61.

The importance of insulating lightning conductors, seems to have been better understood by electricians, than the methods by which it is effected. Some philosophers observe, that the insulation may be effected by "having the iron fastenings of the rod to the wall large and blunt, and covered with two or three folds of woollen cloth steeped in, and covered with melted pitch:"* others, "that the conductor should be fastened to the wall not by iron cramps, but by pieces of wood. If the conductor were quite detached from the building, and supported by wooden posts the distance of one or two feet from the wall, it would be much better."† While others, still, have thought that a more perfect insulation was secured by India-rubber, or by passing the rod through the necks of glass bottles, and more recently, through glass thimbles or rings, cut vertically through the centre. If insulation is effected by thus passing the conductor through glass, it is much better that the glass rings be in two semicircular parts than to have it whole; for experience has proved, that it is far less likely to be broken by the sudden heat and violent expansion of air which always precedes the electric fluid in a lightning discharge. If the lightning rod could pass round or over glass caps, as the telegraphic wires do, it would be better still. With such a mode of insulation, no possible harm can result to the insulator, however powerful the explosion.

* *Encyclopœdia*, vol. viii., p. 647.

† *London Encyclovœdia*, vol. viii., p. 61.

We close our remarks on the construction of lightning conductors, with a quotation from Professor Sturgeon, Superintendent and Lecturer of the Royal Victoria Gallery of Practical Science, Manchester, formerly Lecturer on Experimental Philosophy at the Hon. East India Company's Military Academy, Addiscombe, &c., &c., &c.

"The subject of lightning conductors is a branch of practical electricity of exceedingly high interest, and demands the contemplation of the most profound electricians. Hitherto, however, little more has been attended to than the erection of a pointed rod of iron, without regard to situation, altitude, diameter, inferior termination, or any of those theoretical points essential to the efficacy and protection of the conductors, so as to render it a safeguard to persons and property against the 'most formidable element of nature.'

"Franklin, the inventor of lightning conductors, first proposed, 'for protecting houses, churches, ships, &c., from the stroke of lightning, to fix on the highest parts of these edifices upright rods of iron, made sharp as a needle, and gilt, to prevent rusting; and from the foot of these rods, *a wire down the outside of the building into the ground, or round one of the shrouds of a ship, and down her side, till it reaches the water.* Would not these pointed rods probably draw the electrical fire silently out of a cloud before it came near enough to strike, and thereby secure us from that most sudden and terrible mischief?'"

This philosopher, however, subsequently recommended continuous iron rods, of about half or three-quarters of an inch diameter; which he said "may be fastened to the wall, chimney, &c., with staples of iron. The lightning will not leave the rod, a good conductor, to pass into the wall, a bad conductor, through the staples. It would rather, if any were in the wall, pass out of it into the rod, to get more readily by that conductor into the earth.

"If the building be very large and extensive, two or more rods may be placed at different parts, for greater security.

"Small ragged parts of clouds suspended in the air between the great body of clouds and the earth, often serve as partial conductors for the lightning, which proceeds from one of them to another, and by their help comes within the striking distance of the earth or a building. It therefore strikes through those conductors a building that would otherwise be out of the striking distance.

"Long sharp points communicating with the earth, and presented to such parts of clouds, draw silently from them the fluid they are charged with; these parts of clouds are then attracted to the main cloud, and may leave the distance so great as to be beyond the reach of striking.

"It is therefore that we elevate the upper end of the rod six or eight feet above the highest part of the building, tapering it gradually to a fine sharp point, gilt to prevent its rusting. Thus the pointed rod either prevents a stroke from the cloud, or if a stroke be made, conducts it to the earth with safety to the building.

"The lower end of the rod should enter the earth so deep as to come at the moist part, and if bent under the surface so as to go in a horizontal line six or eight feet from the wall, and then bent again downwards three or four feet, it will prevent damage to any of the stones of the foundation."

Of these instructions of the celebrated Franklin, Prof. Sturgeon remarks, that "had he recommended copper rods instead of iron, and directed them to be kept clear of the building instead of being fastened to the walls with staples of iron, perhaps no better instructions could have been given; as far, at least, as an individual rod is concerned. But besides the injury that buildings may receive from a flash of lightning striking a conductor fixed close to the slates and masonry, from lateral explosions, a conductor consisting of a single branch only might be the means of drawing down destruction to some parts of the building before the lightning reached that conductor. For, were the lightning cloud on one side of the building, and the conductor on the other, the lightning would neither go round nor over the house to arrive at the conductor, unless it met with greater resistance in a direct path, and as the destination of lightning is frequently a greater distance from the cloud, and its path considerably oblique, it is possible that some part of its path might be through a part of the building before it arrived at a lightning rod which formed another part of its path.

"Cases of this kind have occurred, and, consequently, may possibly occur again under similar circumstances; therefore it seems to me that unless lightning conductors be properly placed, and of proper materials and dimensions, they may be the means of causing the most destructive consequences to those buildings they were intended to protect. *It is very seldom indeed that a flash of lightning proceeds in a vertical path; perhaps never.*

"I never yet saw, or heard of, a vertical discharge of lightning; they are frequently very oblique indeed. The lightning which damaged Saint Michael's Church, at Liverpool, last year, was an oblique discharge, and struck the bronze cross at the top of the spire, several feet from its top.

"There is such a display of ignorance in the erection of tall spires, that it is almost a miracle that the whole of them are not destroyed by lightning. The upper clamps and strings of lead, the former uniformly placed at intervals from each other, and the latter wantonly poured into the crevices of the masonry, render the spire a complete chain of alternate links of metal and masonry from top to bottom: the former inviting the lightning to the edifice, and the latter offering facilities for the most destructive explosions. From this very arrangement of the materials in the steeples of Saint Michael's and Saint Martin's at Liverpool, and in the steeple of Brixton Church, have these three steeples been shattered by lightning. If such modes of building tall spires be indispensable to protect them from the power of the wind, conductors are quite as indispensable to protect them from lightning. Three rods (copper best) at equal distances from one another, from the top of the spire to the ground, and united at the top, and by one or two bands below, would secure each spire from lightning on whichever side it approached.

"Lightning rods however numerous about a building, should have a *general metallic union;* they then form a system of conductors in which the force of the lightning would be divided, whichever branch was struck. I have a beautiful experiment to offer to your notice, illustrative of this fact.

'The apparatus represented by fig. 18, consists

FIG. 18.

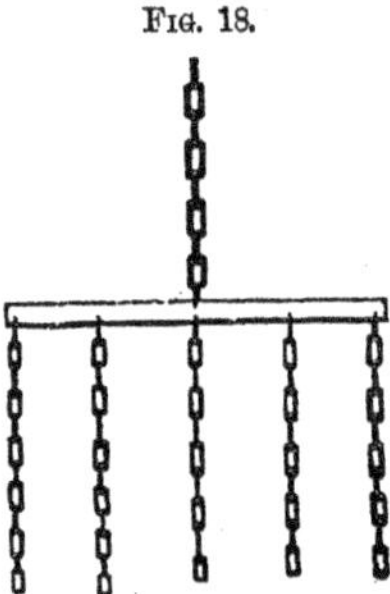

of a series of iron wire chains, so connected as to form a system of conductors of many branches. The chains hang vertically from a horizontal brass wire, and their lower ends rest on a sheet of tin-foil. The brass wire first receives the jars, and the tin-foil carries it from the chains to the outside of the jar. The electric fluid, whilst traversing this circuit, illuminates every chain in the system to the same extent, showing that it is equally divided amongst them; and had there been ten thousand such channels, it would have divided itself amongst the whole of them. This experiment shows two or more interesting facts. It proves that the iron scintillates at every link by an electric discharge through a chain of that metal; and these scintillations discover to us that the fluid occupies, and passes through, every channel in the circuit."*

That we may not omit any information on the subject that may be deemed useful, we shall add Mr. Morgan's method of preventing all possible danger. The plan which Mr. Morgan proposes is, that, whilst a house is being built, "the foundation of each partition wall should be laid on a strip of lead, or a strip should be fastened to the sides of these partition walls. The strips should be two inches wide, and at least a quarter of an inch thick, and closely connected with each other. A perpendicular strip, on each side of the house, should rise from the conductors to the surface of the ground; whence a strip should be continued round the house, and carefully connected with water-pipes, &c. The strips on the sides of the house should then be continued to the roof, which ought to be guarded in the same manner as the foundation. The top should be surrounded by a strip, which should be connected with every edge and prominence, and continued to the summit of each separate chimney." It is particularly

* *Sturgeon's Lectures on Electricity.*

necessary to guard the chimneys; for Mr. Morgan mentions a case in which a house that had been guarded in most respects, according to the preceding directions, except that the chimneys were unprotected, was struck with lightning, which entered by one of the chimneys; here it spent its fury; but the chimneys falling on the roof did considerable damage.

All electricians agree "that security is rendered more perfect by having every piece of metal on the roof in metallic connection with the conductor, and continuous strips of lead built into every wall, and connected to one another by horizontal strips communicating also with the conductor."*

The only objection to this method of protection is the expense. But even this is mainly obviated, by having the conductors so constructed as to run the whole length of the building on the ridge, with branches to the chimneys, and duly elevated above them; and, in case of small buildings, continuing the main rod on the ridge over the roof, down the opposite diagonal corners of the building to the ground; and if the building is large, by having rods extend from the main rod on the ridge over each end of the roof, down the four corners; and having all the conductors united to one another by a perfect metallic union.

Practical Deductions.

1. The conductor should be made of good conducting substance.

* *Encyclopædia Britannica,* vol. viii. p. 647.

2. It should have great electrical capacities; a square rod requires less metal than a round rod.

3. It should be perfectly continuous, *i. e.*, it should have no breaks in the connections; no links or hooks, but a perfect metallic union of every part. If a person should think that a ring of zinc near these connections, improves the appearance of the rod, there can be no objection, though there is no other possible advantage.

4. It should be insulated from the building to be protected, except from such masses of metal as are likely to offer other lines of discharge.

5. It should have numerous lateral points:—one in six or seven feet will answer. The more numerous these points are, the greater the conducting power of the rod. Besides, these lateral points provide for an oblique discharge, each being as good a receiving point as the higher point at the chimney or other prominences. They also guard against a lateral explosion, or a division of the charge, which is liable to happen in case the rod is overcharged, especially if it be fastened to the house with pointed staples; and in case of an upward stroke, the electric fluid being discharged at so many different points, no harm can possibly occur.

6. Its upper extremity should project freely into the air; should be pointed; and may be triangular, somewhat similar to a bayonet; or it may have several branches. The only scientific advantage in having a branching head or point for the superior termination, is this: all the points are not likely to

become blunt at the same time. Some have supposed that the point should be *magnetized;* and little needles, called "*magnets,*" have sometimes been added. But it is difficult to see the practicability of this recent discovery; for most are aware, that magnetized iron or steel soon loses its magnetic influence. But, *is* there any truth or science in this application of magnetism? If there *is*, we confess, that we have not been able to discover it in any experiments in the laboratory; neither can we learn that the subject has even been *mentioned* by any writer *whatever*, on the subject of electricity.

7. The upper termination should be plated with silver or gold, to prevent corrosion.

8. Every branch rod running to chimneys, and other prominences, should have a perfect metallic union with the main rod.

9. In cases where metallic vane-spindles, or other points exist, the conductor may commence from these, and should be applied immediately to the part to be protected, and not at a distance from it; and should be so applied, that a discharge of lightning falling on the general mass, could not possibly find its way to the ground through the building by any circuit of which the conductor did not form a part; that is to say, the conductor should be so carried over the several parts of the building, that the discharge could not fall upon it without being transmitted safely by the conductor. Hence, the rod should run along the whole length of the ridge, and

down to the ground, at least on two sides of the building. If the building is large, it should run down on each corner.

10. Every conductor running to the ground, should terminate sufficiently beneath the surface, to insure moisture in the dryest part of the season. If circumstances permit, it should connect with a spring of water, a drain, or some other conducting channel.

Concluding Observations.

We have seen that electricity is, from various causes, generated and set free in our atmosphere; and that individual clouds, and masses of clouds, are often highly charged with electricity, and insulated by the surrounding air. The earth and the sea are good conductors of electricity; and, generally speaking, their natural electricity is undisturbed. The attraction, therefore, of the electricity of the clouds for the opposite electricity in the earth or the sea, may become so powerful as to break through the resisting medium which intervenes. If the clouds are above a mountain, or rising ground, this discharge of electric matter into the earth is often attended with the fusion of portions of the rocks which crown these exposed summits. If a tree stands in the stratum of air through which the cloud discharges itself, the lightning passes through it, cleaving, and bursting, and damaging it in its passage. If a house obstructs its path, the electricity descends through its walls, and gilded pictures, and finds out any matter, whether organized or unorganized, living or dead, which is placed near its path, and is capable of advancing it on its rapid and breathless errand to the earth. If a living animal grazing, or a human being walking in an open field, intervenes between the overcharged cloud and the ground, the one or the other will become the chosen path of this irresistible foe. If a ship floats under an electrified canopy of vapor, it has less chance of escape than the tree, the house, or the living being.

The only terms upon which we can meet this relentless enemy, is an humble admission of its supreme and irresistible power, and a resolution to give it the freest and the fullest passport through our territory. We must supply it, in short, with a railway of metal, the only species of road upon which it can travel with a suitable speed and a harmless intention. The moment it ceases to find a conducting body, it begins its devastation among imperfect or non-conducting substances, till it again gets into a safe and easy path.

Truly was it an auspicious period when Dr. Franklin raised electricity to the dignity of a science, and connected it with that tremendous agency which had so often terrified the moral, and convulsed the physical world. The thunderbolt had frequently descended from heaven upon its victims; but mortal genius, though it comprehended not the most perfect method of constructing an electrical machine, or a lightning conductor, had now learned to bring it down in chains, to disarm its fury, and to convert it into a useful, and even a friendly element.

After a successful test of the utility of lightning conductors on the house of Mr. West in Philadelphia, with a mind quick to perceive and a heart true to a sense of justice, how natural the congratulations of Mr. Kinersley to Dr. Franklin. "Sir, I most heartily congratulate you on the pleasure you must experience on finding your great and well-grounded expectations so far fulfilled. May this method of security from the destructive violence of one of the most awful powers of nature, meet with such further success, as to induce every good and grateful heart to bless God for the important discovery! May the benefit thereof be diffused over the whole globe! May it extend to the latest posterity of mankind, and make the name of Franklin, like that of Newton, *immortal*."

Upon a review of what has been advanced in the course of these pages, relative to the nature of thunderstorms and the operation of lightning rods, it appears that buildings and other elevations are struck and damaged by lightning, only in consequence of their being points in one of the terminating planes of a great electrical disturbance in the atmosphere; not from any property of attraction for the matter of lightning, inherent in the substances of which such elevations are composed:—that lightning rods remove, by the aptness of their parts, the resistance experienced by the electrical discharge in moving through less perfect conducting matter;

and hence, by allowing a rapid and free neutralization of the opposite electrical powers, they prevent the damage attendant on an obstructed action:—that the operation of such rods, being of a purely passive kind, they can no more be said to invite or draw down lightning upon the buildings to which they are applied, than a rain-pipe can be said to draw down or invite the rain which flows through it:—that such a passive property cannot be fairly adduced as an argument against their general use:—that since lightning rods only operate in transmitting as much electricity as falls on them, they cannot be prejudicial to buildings, but must, on the contrary, by a rapid annihilation either of the whole or a part of the force in action, necessarily contribute to security:—that lightning, being nothing more than the electrical discharge moving through bad conducting matter, under an explosive form, the tendency of a lightning rod is to deprive the discharge of this form from the instant it falls on the point of the rod, and by converting it into an evanescent current, through matter calculated to assist its progress, to annihilate it as lightning altogether.

In the treatment of this question, it was not possible to avoid a frequent appeal to electrical action, on the great scale of nature. If, therefore, the remarkable instances quoted, of lightning striking on buildings and ships, should appear to be somewhat numerous, and to be treated of in too great detail, yet it must be recollected, that it is only by pursuing such a course that we can hope to arrive at deductions worthy of confidence. Hence it is, that in the progress of these inquiries we have been led to adhere carefully to a series of well-authenticated facts, and by keeping strictly within the safe path of inductive science, we have endeavored to throw some further light on a subject of very great public importance, which has not been generally or fully appreciated. With respect to certain prejudiced views and opinions which have been entertained of the operation of lightning rods, we trust to have made it appear that such opinions are founded on no sound basis whatever, and that a judicious application of pointed conductors, both on land and at sea, is not only desirable, but is, in a great variety of cases, quite essential to the preservation of buildings and ships from the ravages of lightning.

THE END.

www.ingramcontent.com/pod-product-compliance
Lightning Source LLC
LaVergne TN
LVHW011217110826
845150LV00006B/1447

9781425517250